KV-030-564

LUCY-ANN BUCKLEY

COMBATTING DISABILITY HARASSMENT AT WORK

Human Rights in Practice

BRISTOL
UNIVERSITY
PRESS

First published in Great Britain in 2022 by

Bristol University Press
University of Bristol
1–9 Old Park Hill
Bristol
BS2 8BB
UK
t: +44 (0)117 374 6645
e: bup-info@bristol.ac.uk

Details of international sales and distribution partners are available at
bristoluniversitypress.co.uk

British Library Cataloguing in Publication Data
A catalogue record for this book is available from the British Library

ISBN 978-1-5292-2378-1 hardcover
ISBN 978-1-5292-2379-8 ePub
ISBN 978-1-5292-2380-4 ePdf

Cover design: blu inc
Front cover image: iStock/Martin Barraud
Bristol University Press uses environmentally responsible
print partners.
Printed in Great Britain by CPI Group (UK) Ltd, Croydon,
CR0 4YY

To Diarmuid and Aoibhín

Contents

List of Cases   vi

List of Legislation   x

List of International Instruments   xi

List of Tables   xii

List of Abbreviations   xiii

Notes on the Author   xv

Acknowledgements   xvi

one   Introduction   1

two   The Human Rights Framework   21

three   Barriers to Effective National Implementation 59

four   Disability Harassment in Ireland   78

five   The Irish Legal Framework in Practice   97

six   Meeting the Global Challenge: Lessons from   141
         Experience

seven   Conclusion   169

Index   178

List of Cases

A Clerical Officer v A Public Service Employer ADJ-00018924

A Complainant v A Company DEC-E2002-014

A Complainant v A Food Processing Company Limited DEC-E2012-064

A Complainant v A Named Development Association & FÁS DEC-E2013-057

A Complainant v A Private Security Firm DEC-E2011-231

A Complainant v A Respondent DEC-E2013-128

A Complainant v A Third Level Institution DEC-E2012-160

A Customer Care Representative v A Provider of Outsourced Customer Support to a Mobile Phone Operator DEC-E2016-092

An Electrical Engineer v An Electricity Company ADJ-00016282

An Employee v A Chain of Retail Stores ADJ-00003084

An Employee v An Employer DEC-E2016-005

An Employee v A Government Department ADJ-00015888

An Employee v A Healthcare Company ADJ-00017070

A Female Employee v A Printing Company DEC-E2008-022

A Government Department v A Worker EDA094

An IT Systems Support Officer v A Hospital ADJ-00021831

A Manager of an English Language School v An Institute of Technology DEC–E2007–019

A Nurse v A Hospital ADJ-00000278

A Retail Manager v A Supermarket Chain ADJ-00005949

A Security Guard v A Security Firm ADJ-00018217

A Software Engineer v A Respondent DEC-E2012-195

A Training Co-ordinator/Instructor v A Training and Rehabilitation Organisation ADJ-00017677

A Worker v An Employer DEC-E2012-132

A Worker v A Government Department DEC-E2016-116

A Worker v A Restaurant DEC-E2012-161

Alajos Kiss v Hungary 38832/06 [2010] ECHR 692 (20 May 2010)

Bigaeva against Greece 26713/05 [2011] ECHR 2164 (2 December 2011)

C-188/15, *Asma Bougnaoui and Association de Défense des Droits de l'Homme (ADDH) v Micropole SA* [2017] ECLI:EU:C:2017:204

C-395/15, *Mohamed Daouidi v Bootes Plus SL, Fondo de Garantía Salarial, Ministerio Fiscal* [2016] ECLI:EU:C:2016:917

Carvalho Pinto de Sousa v Portugal 17484/15 [2017] ECHR 719 (25 July 2017)

Case C-13/05, *Chacón Navas v Eurest Colectividades SA* [2006] ECLI:EU:C:2006:456

Case C-157/15, *Samira Achbita and Centrum voor Gelijkheid van Kansen en voor Racismebestrijding v G4S Secure Solutions NV* [2016] ECLI:C:2016:382 [2017] ECLI:EU:C:2017:203

Case C-306/06, *Coleman v Attridge Law* [2008] ECR I-5603

Case C-354/13, *FOA Acting on Behalf of Karsten Kaltoft* [2014] ECLI:EU:C:2014:2463

Case C-363/12, *Z v A Government Department, the Board of Management of a Community School* [2014] ECLI:EU:C:2014:159

Case C-443/15, *David L Parris v Trinity College Dublin and Others* [2016] ECLI:EU:C:2016:897

Case C-83/14, *CHEZ Razpredelenie Bulgaria*, ECLI:EU:C:2015:480

Cementation Skanska (Formerly Kvaerner Cementation) v Carroll DWT0425

Colgan v Boots Ireland Ltd DEC–E2010-008

Conlon v Intel Ireland Ltd DEC-E2014-100

County Louth VEC v Don Johnson EDA0712

Eithne McDermott v Connacht Gold Co-operative Society Ltd DEC-E2011-147

European Court of Human Rights, 'Case Relating to Certain Aspects of the Laws on the Use of Languages in Education in Belgium. (Preliminary Objection and Merits)' (1972) 45 International Law Reports 114

Food and Beverage Assistant v A Hotel ADJ-00012892

Glor v Switzerland 13444/04 [2009] ECHR 2181 (30 April 2009)

Hannon v First Direct Logistics Limited DEC-E2011-066

Harrington v Natus Nicolet Ireland Limited DEC-E2012-197

Hennessy v Crowe UD812/2013

Hurley v County Cork VEC EDA1124

Ilona Latvenaite v Rocliffe Ltd and ABP (Anglo Beef Processors Ireland t/a ABP) DEC-E2014-038

Joined Cases C-335/11 and C-337/11, *HK Danmark, Acting on Behalf of Jette Ring v Dansk almennyttigt Boligselskab and HK Danmark, Acting on Behalf of Lone Skouboe Werge v Dansk Arbejdsgiverforening, Acting on Behalf of Pro Display A/S (Ring and Skouboe Werge)* [2013] ECLI:EU:C:3013: 222

Josef Walkowaik v O'Leary International Limited DEC-E2016-022

Kiyutin v Russia 2700/10 [2011] ECHR 439 (10 March 2011)

Kristina Blumberga v Kilbush Nurseries Ltd DEC-E2015-165

Maher v HSE South DEC-E2016-144

McCarthy v ISS Ireland Limited (Trading as ISS Facility Services) & Anor [2018] IECA 287

Mr A v An Employer DEC-E2010-075

Mr A v A Hospital DEC-E2012-192

Mr L v A Manufacturing Company DEC-E2005-054

Ms A v A Charitable Organisation DEC-E2011-049

Ms A v A Contract Cleaning Company DEC–E2004–068

Ms Bridget Connolly v Health Service Executive DEC-E2008-061

Ms Josephine Riney v Donegal ETB, Formerly Co. Donegal VEC DEC- E2015-139

Ms Karen Bradford v Public Appointments Service DEC-E2007-02

Mullen v Smurfit Kappa Ireland Limited DEC-E2012-176

N.B. v Slovakia 29518/10 [2012] ECHR 991 (12 June 2012)

Nano Nagle School v Daly [2018] IECA 11 (31 January 2018)

Negovanović and Others v Serbia (Application No. 29907/16 and Three Others, 25 January 2022)

Roksana Wypch v Pagewell Concessions (Ilac) Ltd Trading as Euro 50 Store, Ilac Centre DEC-E2015-080

Sacha v Seaview Hotel Ltd DEC-E2016-055

Sally Dowling v Debenhams Plc DEC-E2017-085

Sea and Shore Safety Services Ltd v Amanda Byrne EDA143

Sidabras and Dziautas v Lithuania 55480/00;59330/00 [2004] ECHR 395 (27 July 2004)

Tomasz Zalewski (Applicant/Appellant) v An Adjudication Officer, the Workplace Relations Commission, Ireland and the Attorney General (Respondents) and *Buywise Discount Store Limited (Notice Party)* [2021] IESC 29

Unite the Union v Nailard [2018] EWCA Civ 1203

V.C. v Slovakia 18968/07 [2011] ECHR 1888 (8 November 2011)

Vento v Chief Constable of West Yorkshire Police (No. 2) [2002] EWCA Civ 1871

Victor Kings Oluebube v CPL Solutions Limited t/a Flexsource Recruitment [2020] ADJ-00024254

Worker v An Employer DEC-E2012-132

List of Legislation

Americans with Disabilities Act 1990

Civil Rights Act 1964

Council Directive 2000/78/EC of 27 November 2000 Establishing a General Framework for Equal Treatment in Employment and Occupation [2000] OJ L 303

Disability Discrimination Act 1995

Employment Equality Acts 1998–2021

Employment Tribunals Act 1996

Equal Opportunity Act 2010 (Vict)

Equality Act 2010

European Union (Withdrawal Agreement) Act 2018

Irish Human Rights and Equality Commission Act 2014

Prohibition of Incitement to Hatred Act 1989

Sex Discrimination Act 1984 (Cth)

Workplace Relations Act 2015

List of International Instruments

Agreement on the withdrawal of the United Kingdom of Great Britain and Northern Ireland from the European Union and the European Atomic Energy Community, 2019: Protocol on Northern Ireland

Beijing Declaration and Platform for Action

Convention on the Elimination of All Forms of Discrimination against Women

Convention on the Elimination of All Forms of Racial Discrimination

Convention on the Rights of the Child

Convention on the Rights of Persons with Disabilities

ILO Violence and Harassment Convention 2019 (No. 190)

ILO Violence and Harassment Recommendation 2019 (No. 206)

International Convention on Economic, Social and Cultural Rights

Protocol to the African Charter on Human and People's Rights on the Rights of Women in Africa (Maputo Protocol)

List of Tables

5.1	Case overview	106
5.2	Statutory provisions cited in unsuccessful claims in relation to alleged harassment	107
5.3	Reasons cited for failure of claim by adjudicating body	109
5.4	Reasons cited for success of claim	117
5.5	Overall party representation	121
5.6	Frequency of citation in cases where parties had or did not have legal or other representation	122
5.7	Unsuccessful claims by type of discrimination alleged	124
5.8	Unsuccessful claims by type of harassment alleged	125

List of Abbreviations

ADA	Americans with Disabilities Act 1990
AHRC	Australian Human Rights Commission
BSAS	British Social Attitudes Survey
CEDAW	Convention on the Elimination of All Forms of Discrimination against Women
CERD	Convention on the Elimination of All Forms of Racial Discrimination
CESCR	Committee on Economic, Social and Cultural Rights
CJEU	Court of Justice of the European Union
CRC	Convention on the Rights of the Child
CRPD	Convention on the Rights of Persons with Disabilities
CSO	Central Statistics Office (Ireland)
ECHR	European Convention on Human Rights
EEA	Employment Equality Acts 1998–2021 (Ireland)
EEOC	Equal Employment Opportunity Commission (US)
EHRC	Equality and Human Rights Commission (UK)
ET	Equality Tribunal (Ireland)
EU	European Union
FED	Framework Employment Directive (Council Directive 2000/78/EC)
ICESCR	International Covenant on Economic, Social and Cultural Rights
ILO	International Labour Organization
ILO Convention	ILO Violence and Harassment Convention 2019 (No. 190)
LC	Labour Court (Ireland)
ONS	Office for National Statistics (UK)

UN	United Nations
US	United States
WRC	Workplace Relations Commission (Ireland)

Notes on the Author

Lucy-Ann Buckley is Associate Professor in Law at the University of Galway, specializing in equality law. She has published widely on such issues as reasonable accommodation (adjustment) for persons with disabilities, sexual harassment of women with disabilities and gender equality in employment law. From 2018 to 2020, she acted as an expert advisor to the States of Guernsey in relation to the development of new multi-ground equality legislation.

Acknowledgements

I am deeply grateful to my excellent colleagues, Shivaun Quinlivan, Caterina Gardiner and Anna-Louise Hinds, for their encouragement, support and constructive feedback on drafts of this book. I would also like to thank Brodie O'Toole for her research assistance and her help in preparing this manuscript. Finally, I would like to express my gratitude to the anonymous referees for their thoughtful and helpful comments on both the proposal for this book and the completed manuscript.

ONE

Introduction

1.1 Introduction

Persons with disabilities experience high levels of harassment[1] and are particularly exposed to intersectional harassment based on multiple characteristics, such as race, gender and age.[2] However, while sexual and racial harassment have received considerable attention from legal scholars, there has been little in-depth analysis of disability harassment law.[3] There has also been surprisingly little discussion of the human rights framework, the effectiveness of legal measures seeking to address disability harassment or the reasons for the success or failure of disability harassment claims. While scholarly articles have evaluated the operation of disability equality law in specific areas, they do not generally address harassment,[4] are limited in the scope of their studies[5] or do not offer disaggregated

---

[1] See, generally, Equality and Human Rights Commission (EHRC), 'Hidden in plain sight: inquiry into disability-related harassment' (EHRC 2011).

[2] Linda R. Shaw, Fong Chan and Brian T. McMahon, 'Intersectionality and disability harassment' (2011) 55 *Rehabilitation Counseling Bulletin*, 82.

[3] For an exception, see Mark C. Weber, *Disability Harassment* (New York University Press 2007).

[4] See, for example, Ruth Colker, 'Winning and losing under the Americans with Disabilities Act' (2001) 62 *Ohio State Law Journal*, 239.

[5] See, for example, Graeme Lockwood, Claire Henderson and Graham Thornicroft, 'Challenging mental health discrimination in employment' (2012–2013) 17 *Journal of Workplace Rights*, 137.

data.[6] The connections between disability harassment and other characteristics, such as race and gender, also remain under-examined from a legal perspective, despite a broader social science literature and increasing attention from policy actors.[7]

This book addresses these gaps. Focusing on legal measures to combat disability harassment at work, the book sets disability harassment in its human rights framework and addresses the lack of empirical information by examining the operation of disability harassment law in one jurisdiction: Ireland. It outlines barriers to the effective operation of disability harassment provisions and explores the capacity of harassment law to address intersectional forms of harassment.

The book begins with an overview, outlining both the prevalence of disability harassment and its impact in the work context. Chapter One also highlights the connections between disability harassment and other characteristics, and explains the importance of intersectional approaches to discrimination.

Chapter Two outlines the human rights framework for addressing disability harassment, focusing particularly on the United Nations (UN) Convention on the Rights of Persons with Disabilities (CRPD) and, in the European Union (EU) context, the Framework Employment Directive (FED),[8] with additional attention to the recent International Labour Organization (ILO) Violence and Harassment Convention 2019.[9] This chapter emphasizes the significance of distinctions

---

[6] See, for example, Graeme Lockwood and Vidushi Marda, 'Harassment in the workplace: the legal context' (2014) 31 *Jurisprudence*, 667.

[7] For recent reports addressing harassment of persons with disabilities, see Rosario Grima Algora and Purna Sen, *Sexual Harassment against Women with Disabilities in the Work Place and on Campus* (UN Women 2020); Australian Human Rights Commission (AHRC), *Respect@Work: Sexual Harassment National Inquiry Report* (AHRC 2020).

[8] Council Directive 2000/78/EC of 27 November 2000 Establishing a General Framework for Equal Treatment in Employment and Occupation [2000] OJ L 303.

[9] Violence and Harassment Convention 2019 (No. 190).

between the CRPD and the FED, as EU states may comply with the FED yet fail to comply fully with the CRPD. This may lead to important gaps in protection for persons with disabilities.

Chapter Three outlines a wide range of social and structural barriers that may discourage legal claims, and explores the available data on the effectiveness of equality legislation in practice. Even where national measures are adopted, it is unclear how effective they are in practice, as states have generally failed to gather information on the operation of disability harassment law. There are clear indicators that harassment law in general is often less effective than might be hoped – for instance, recent UK and Australian reports highlight serious issues with legislative efficacy in the related context of sexual harassment,[10] and many difficulties discussed in both reports apply more broadly to harassment generally. These reports must also be seen against a backdrop of research that identifies widespread general barriers to the enforcement of equality law,[11] as well as disability-specific and intersectional barriers that may limit access to justice.[12]

Chapter Four outlines the social and legal context for disability harassment in Ireland. It highlights similarities between disability harassment rates in Ireland and internationally, and outlines the key legal provisions on disability harassment at work contained in the Employment Equality Acts 1998–2021 (EEA). The chapter argues that while Irish law complies with EU requirements under the FED, it fails to satisfy the requirements of the CRPD in relation to intersectional discrimination.

---

[10] Women and Equalities Committee, *Sexual Harassment in the Workplace* (HC 2017–19, 725-I); AHRC, in note 7.

[11] See, for instance, Bradley A. Areheart, 'Organizational justice and antidiscrimination' (2020) 104 *Minnesota Law Review*, 1921.

[12] See, for instance, Lucy-Ann Buckley, 'Women with disabilities: forever on the edge of #MeToo?', in Ann M. Noel and David B. Oppenheimer (eds), *Globalization of the #MeToo Movement* (Fastcase and Full Court Press 2020).

Chapter Five evaluates the operation of Irish law in practice, considering primarily its 'curative' effectiveness (the extent to which law rectifies a previous injustice).[13] Analysing all available disability harassment decisions under the EEA from 1998 to 2020, it finds that very few cases go to hearing and that the success rate for claims is extremely low. It then explores the reasons for the success and failure of claims, the kinds of remedies awarded, and the implications of these findings. It concludes by arguing that, notwithstanding the EEA's theoretical capacity to address much work-related disability harassment, it has not been curatively effective in practice.

Chapter Six considers the more general application of the Irish findings, as well as possible solutions to the problems identified, including the need for positive employer duties and greater transparency. The book concludes, in Chapter Seven, by highlighting the difficulty in achieving effective vindication of human rights at the national level. The Irish findings echo the available data from other jurisdictions, raising broader concerns for the effectiveness of disability harassment legislation. While some issues identified in Ireland may be context-specific, the fundamental concern – the effectiveness of national measures vindicating the human rights of persons with disabilities – is internationally relevant. Chapter Seven therefore again emphasizes the importance of monitoring and positive employer duties in ensuring that national legislation is effective in practice.

It is important to note some limitations. First, the empirical study in the book focuses on one jurisdiction. Ireland is a useful exemplar, as it is an EU member state that has also ratified the CRPD and that has adopted very comprehensive harassment provisions, including a very broad definition of disability. Protection for human rights should therefore (in theory) be

---

[13] Anthony Allott, 'The effectiveness of laws' (1981) 15 *Valparaiso University Law Review*, 229, 234.

very strong. The requirements of EU law ensure a degree of comparability with other EU member states (and former member states – even following Brexit, the FED is part of the legacy of EU law incorporated into domestic law in the UK). Second, the book focuses on disability harassment *at work*. While it makes some reference to disability harassment in other contexts (for instance, hate crime, education and access to services), it does not explore these in detail. The scope is driven by practical considerations, such as the availability and scale of data, and the capacity of a short monograph. Third, in considering the human rights framework, the book focuses primarily on the CRPD and the FED as most relevant to the Irish context, with some reference to the ILO Convention on Violence and Harassment. The book does not address other human rights instruments in detail, either because their regional focus is irrelevant to Ireland/Europe, because they are less relevant to disability or employment, or because the rights they address are replicated or surpassed by later, more focused instruments.

Finally, a note on terminology. The language used in the context of disability is often contested, with particular attention focused on the 'person-first' or 'identity-first' debate. In person-first language (such as 'persons with disabilities'), the focus is on the personhood of the individual, rather than their impairment or condition.[14] By contrast, identity-first language (such as 'disabled people') recognizes both that a condition may be an inseparable part of someone's identity[15] and that disability results from the impact of socially constructed barriers, including attitudinal barriers, rather than from a condition or impairment as such.[16]

---

[14] Paul David Harpur, *Ableism at Work: Disablement and Hierarchies of Impairment* (Cambridge University Press 2019), 5.

[15] Dana S. Dunn and Erin E. Andrews, 'Person-first and identity-first language' (2015) 70 *The American Psychologist*, 255, 257.

[16] Anna Lawson and Mark Priestley, 'The social model of disability: questions for law and legal scholarship?', in Peter Blanck and Eilionóir Flynn (eds),

In the context of disability harassment, person-first language emphasizes the humanity of the victim(s), counteracting the 'othering' on which much disability harassment is based.[17] By contrast, identity-first language conveys the disabling effects of harassment, for instance, as a barrier to employment and social participation. The CRPD, which is a key focus of this book, is notable for its use of person-first language. For this reason, this book generally employs person-first language (other than in direct quotations),[18] while acknowledging that different usages may be preferred by others or in relation to certain conditions. For similar reasons, the term 'psychosocial disability' is used rather than referring to a variety of mental conditions and impairments. Although the CRPD does not itself refer to psychosocial disabilities, the term has been consistently used by the Committee on the Rights of Persons with Disabilities (CRPD Committee) in its general comments in preference to the term 'mental disability'.[19]

1.2 The nature of disability harassment

Disability harassment may be broadly defined as intimidating, humiliating, insulting or demeaning behaviour related to disability, which is unwelcome to the victim.[20] The form of disability harassment may vary and includes physical acts, spoken words, gestures and the display or circulation of written words or images by electronic or other means. Disability

---

Routledge Handbook of Disability Law and Human Rights (Taylor and Francis 2016), 7.

[17] See Section 1.2.

[18] This primarily applies to UK sources, where identity-first language is generally preferred (see Lawson and Priestly, in note 16, 7).

[19] For a full discussion, see Harpur, in note 14, 6.

[20] This definition draws on the CRPD and the FED, as discussed in Chapter Two.

harassment creates a hostile environment for the victim, either at work or in other contexts, such as education, healthcare, access to goods or services, or sport.

In an in-depth report on disability harassment outside the work context, the UK Equality and Human Rights Commission (EHRC) summarized a wide variety of harassment described by persons with disabilities during its research. Examples included:

> being ignored or overlooked; stared at; called names; asked intrusive questions, offered offensive advice, patronising comments or jokes; threatened or actual physical harassment including invasion of personal space, touching, pushing, being spat at or hit or being the target of thrown objects; sexual harassment and assault; damage to property; and actual or attempted theft or fraud.[21]

Similar instances are described in the employment context by Koch et al in the broader context of 'mistreatment' at work,[22] as well as by Weber in his leading study of disability harassment in the US.[23]

While the forms of disability harassment are wide-ranging, it is commonly thought to stem from exclusion and stigmatization. Bagenstos notes that persons with disabilities experience systemic obstacles to social participation, based on prejudice, stereotyping and neglect. However, while these factors may appear distinct, Bagenstos contends that they are connected insofar as they are all likely to be experienced by people who differ too much from the prevailing social

---

[21] EHRC, in note 1, 66.

[22] Lynn C. Koch and others, 'On-the-job treatment of employees with disabilities: a grounded theory investigation' (2021) *Rehabilitation Counseling Bulletin*, 1, 7.

[23] Weber, in note 3, ch 1.

norm.[24] Prejudice and stereotyping may be closely connected with disability harassment, as both disability in general and specific kinds of disabilities may be socially stigmatized due to ignorance or assumptions regarding their nature and effects.[25] Weber locates harassment in the othering of persons with disabilities and the imposition of stigma by those with authority or 'practical power'.[26] This othering – which Weber describes as a refusal or inability to accept those who are considered abnormal[27] – both derives from and perpetuates social exclusion. Social structures, attitudes and environments lead to the widespread exclusion and screening out of persons with disabilities. As persons with disabilities are less visible, they are perceived as different, and this perceived difference causes discomfort in others, leading to ridicule or abuse that causes further exclusion. Disability harassment, like other forms of harassment, is therefore connected to exclusion, dominance and the preservation of strength and privileges.[28]

---

[24] Samuel R. Bagenstos, 'Subordination, stigma, and "disability"' (2000) 86 *Virginia Law Review*, 397, 436–7.

[25] See, for example, Katrina Scior, 'Toward understanding intellectual disability stigma: introduction', in Katrina Scior and Shirli Werner (eds), *Intellectual Disability and Stigma: Stepping Out from the Margins* (Palgrave Macmillan 2016); Harpur, in note 14, 4–17.

[26] Weber, in note 3, 2.

[27] Ibid, 2–3.

[28] Ibid, 5. By comparison, both sociocultural theories and organizational theories of sexual harassment emphasize the role of gender-related power differentials. See Afroditi Pina, Theresa A. Gannon and Benjamin Saunders, 'An overview of the literature on sexual harassment: perpetrator, theory, and treatment issues' (2009) 14 *Aggression and Violent Behavior*, 126. For a discussion of othering in the context of racial harassment, see Ashleigh Shelby Rosette et al, 'Intersectionality: connecting experiences of gender with race at work' (2018) 38 *Research in Organizational Behavior*, 1.

There are clear intersections between disability hate crime and disability harassment. Hate crime can be understood as 'criminal acts committed with a bias motive',[29] such as prejudice based on race, religion, disability, sexual orientation or other characteristics. Like harassment, it clearly relies on the othering of the target group and can be understood as a form of social exclusion and a barrier to social participation. It therefore both reflects and reinforces social hierarchy.[30] There may also be an overlap between hate crime and harassment, as some forms of harassment (such as assault or sexual violence) may also constitute criminal offences. Both hate crime and harassment may have a profound and long-lasting psychological effect on the victim.[31] However, harassment may encompass many instances of behaviour that are not criminal in nature, such as the use of demeaning or insulting language or gestures,[32] or the circulation of images outside the scope of criminal law. Disability harassment as discussed in this book is limited to the employment context and does not typically constitute a hate crime.

1.3 Disability harassment and intersectionality

It is particularly important to consider disability harassment in light of intersectional theory. Intersectional analysis casts new light on the prevalence of disability harassment and its interaction with other forms of harassment, particularly racial and sexual harassment, but also harassment based on age, sexual orientation and other characteristics.

---

[29] Organization for Security and Co-operation in Europe/Office for Democratic Institutions and Human Rights, *Hate Crime Laws: A Practical Guide* (OSCE/ODIHR 2009), 1.

[30] Jennifer Schweppe, 'What is a hate crime?' (2021) 7 *Cogent Social Sciences*, 5.

[31] EHRC, in note 1, 73, 93.

[32] It should be noted, however, that 'hate speech' may be a criminal offence in some jurisdictions.

At its most basic, intersectional discrimination refers to less favourable treatment or disadvantage based on the combined effect of different characteristics. The term 'intersectionality' was coined by Crenshaw,[33] who drew on previous work by other Black feminists to highlight the unique experiences and harms disadvantaging Black women. Fredman highlights that intersectionality may be conceptualized in different ways, with such terminology as 'multiple discrimination', 'cumulative discrimination', 'intersectional discrimination' and 'compound discrimination' often used interchangeably, though they also have distinct meanings.[34] This book focuses on two concepts: on the one hand, 'multiple discrimination' refers to different forms of disadvantage, arising from different characteristics, at the same or different times (for instance, being subjected to both racial and disability harassment); on the other, 'intersectional discrimination' refers to harm that results from the intertwined effects of two or more characteristics.[35] A commonly cited example is a restriction on headscarves in the workplace, which limits the ability of Muslim women to participate in employment, though not that of Muslim men or non–Muslim women. Muslim women are therefore subjected to a disadvantage that other groups are not, based on a combination of characteristics. Thus, as Atrey notes, 'intersectionality represents the complexity of disadvantage

---

[33] Kimberlé Crenshaw, 'Demarginalizing the intersection of race and sex: a black feminist critique of antidiscrimination doctrine, feminist theory and antiracist politics' (1989) *University of Chicago Legal Forum*, 139.

[34] Directorate-General for Justice and Consumers (European Commission), European Network of Legal Experts in Gender Equality and Non-discrimination and Sandra Fredman, *Intersectional Discrimination in EU Gender Equality and Non-discrimination Law* (Publications Office of the European Union 2016), 7.

[35] The distinction between multiple and intersectional discrimination identified here draws on the conceptualization of the CRPD Committee, discussed in Section 2.3.

people suffer when they belong to two or more vulnerable groups'.[36]

Intersectional theory highlights problems with what Crenshaw terms 'single axis' discrimination,[37] that is, the requirement that actionable discrimination should be based on a single protected characteristic. Single axis theory assumes that key aspects of personal identity and experience can be scrutinized in isolation, rather than holistically. It may also overlook key experiential differences between cohorts of the same group: for example, the experiences of women and men with disabilities may be very different, but the experiences of women with psychosocial conditions may also differ from those of women with mobility impairments, and the experiences of Black, Brown or minority ethnic women with disabilities may differ from those of White women with disabilities. As Fredman notes, a single axis approach overlooks the importance of power relations in creating hierarchy and social domination.[38] This is because some characteristics are indicators of privilege, while others are markers of disadvantage, and the convergence or interaction of these markers may result in significant differences in experience and power status.

In relation to harassment, intersectional theory has received most attention in the context of gender and race. For instance, Rosette et al have highlighted distinctive stereotypes, experiences and treatment based on specific intersections of gender and race in the context of sexual harassment. They contend that women with intersectional identities are othered in particular ways that increase the psychological distance between members of the majority group and the intersectional

---

[36] Shreya Atrey, 'Introduction: intersectionality from equality to human rights', in Shreya Atrey and Peter Dunne (eds), *Intersectionality and Human Rights Law* (Hart Publishing 2020), 1.

[37] Crenshaw, in note 33.

[38] Directorate-General for Justice and Consumers (European Commission) et al, in note 34, 8.

minority.[39] Similarly, it has been noted that veiled Muslim women are at increased risk of street harassment due to a complex range of factors that include gender, religion, cultural identity, (frequent) immigrant status and their Muslim dress code, which readily marks them out as 'soft' targets.[40]

Intersections with disability have also received attention. In the UK, for example, the EHRC found that persons with disabilities were often targets for harassment because of intersectional aspects of their identity, such as age, race, religion, gender, sexual orientation, or disability type.[41] However, it must be noted that disability is highly heterogeneous, and the type of disability (or a combination of disabilities) can increase the general risk of harassment, the form that harassment takes and the potential for intersectional impact. For example, a distinction is often drawn between disabilities that are 'visible' (that is, apparent to an observer) and those that are 'invisible' or 'hidden' (that is, not immediately apparent). While the distinction is often more nuanced,[42] the visibility of an impairment can be significant in relation to harassment. A person with a noticeable impairment may be more readily identified as a target, but some individuals with hidden disabilities may also be harassed *because* their condition is not immediately apparent.[43] Social understandings of disability are often limited (for instance, it may be assumed that all persons with disabilities will use wheelchairs). Consequently,

---

[39] Rosette et al, in note 28.

[40] Hannah Mason-Bish and Irene Zempi, 'Misogyny, racism, and Islamophobia: street harassment at the intersections' (2018) 14 *Feminist Criminology*, 540.

[41] Chih Hoong Sin, Annie Hedges, Chloe Cook, Nina Mguni and Natasha Comber, *Disabled People's Experiences of Targeted Violence and Hostility* (EHRC 2009).

[42] Michael J. Prince, 'Persons with invisible disabilities and workplace accommodation: findings from a scoping literature review' (2017) 46 *Journal of Vocational Rehabilitation*, 75.

[43] EHRC, in note 1, 90.

some persons with hidden disabilities may be harassed because others believe they are receiving benefits to which they are not entitled.

Many hidden conditions are also stigmatized and may be especially likely to lead to harassment if known. These particularly include psychosocial disabilities, which are often the subject of negative perceptions and stereotypes.[44] Many persons with hidden disabilities may therefore be very hesitant to disclose their disabilities in the employment context.[45] Other highly stigmatized disabilities include intellectual disabilities, which are also the subject of commonly accepted negative stereotypes that have led to widespread social exclusion and breaches of human rights.[46] In this sense, as Harpur notes, there is often a 'hierarchy of impairment'.[47] Both psychosocial and intellectual disabilities have been the subject of not only extremely negative stereotyping, but also specific, highly pejorative language, both within the medical profession and in common usage.[48] This results not only in increased exposure to disability harassment, but also in specific forms of abuse. The problem is exacerbated by reduced access to remedies, as negative stereotyping also affects both the ability to make complaints (due to legal or other systemic barriers) and the credibility accorded to complainants.[49]

From an intersectional point of view, Shaw et al's detailed analysis of Equal Employment Opportunity Commission (EEOC) cases in the US identified unique combinations of characteristics that significantly impacted the chances of experiencing disability harassment.[50] Examining the interaction of gender, race/ethnicity, age and disability, they found that

---

[44] See, for example, Harpur, in note 14, 12.

[45] Prince, in note 42, 80.

[46] Scior, in note 25, 5.

[47] Harpur, in note 14, 15.

[48] Scior, in note 25, 4.

[49] Buckley, in note 12, 427–8.

[50] Shaw et al, in note 2.

gender was the most significant predictor of harassment, followed by the type of impairment. Individuals with behavioural impairments had the highest rate of harassment allegations, followed by sensory and neurological impairments, and then physical impairments. Race was the next most significant predictor, followed by age.

The intersection of disability and gender particularly affects the prevalence of sexual harassment.[51] However, women with disabilities are also exposed to specific forms of gender-based violence.[52] While some forms of intersectional sexual harassment and gender-based violence (such as forcible undressing by male staff) are generally restricted to medical or institutional settings, others may arise in a work setting. These include: commenting about, interfering with or denying access to mobility or communication aids, hygiene facilities, or assistive technologies; forcibly moving a woman's wheelchair or creating physical barriers to restrict her movements; and asking intrusive questions about the sexual activities, preferences or capacities of women with disabilities.[53] Many of these instances (such as restricting movement) would not commonly be seen as 'sexual' in nature, yet may clearly have a sexual dimension as a form of controlling behaviour. Thus, a recent report by UN Women found that 'the bodies of women with disabilities are often deemed to belong to others, to be public property, such that decision-making is removed from the person concerned, including about whether, when and how to control contact'.[54] Construing harassment of this kind as solely either 'disability' harassment or 'sexual' harassment misses key qualitative aspects of both the experience and the harm caused.

---

[51] See Section 1.4.

[52] Catalina Devandas Aguilar, *Report of the Special Rapporteur on the Rights of Persons with Disabilities on Disability-Inclusive Policies* (United Nations General Assembly 2016), 31–2.

[53] For a detailed discussion, see Buckley, in note 12, 427–9.

[54] Grima Algora and Sen, in note 7, 13.

Gender and sexuality may also interact with disability harassment in other ways, where disability affects the appearance of gender conformity. Recent work by Barnett found intersections between gender, sexuality and disability in the harassment of adults on the autism spectrum. Perpetrators of harassment commonly read the participants' disability characteristics as indicating gender or sexual variance from the heterosexual 'norm' and humiliated them as a result. Barnett suggests that 'deviation of comportment is more closely policed than deviation of physical functioning'.[55] She gives the example of a person who was perceived as female (though not identifying as such) being harassed for not walking in a sufficiently 'feminine' way due to dyspraxia.

In summary, intersectionality impacts not only the frequency with which harassment may occur, but also the form that it may take. Intersectional harassment may constitute a 'synergistic' form of discrimination, which is qualitatively different to harassment based on a single characteristic. This qualitative difference in treatment derives from the specific mix of social and cultural assumptions that attaches to members of the intersecting group.

1.4 Prevalence of disability harassment

It is difficult to give exact figures for the prevalence of disability harassment or the various intersectional forms of harassment that persons with disabilities may be subject to, including sexual and racial harassment. Reporting rates for harassment generally (including sexual harassment) are notoriously low,[56] and in

---

[55] Jessica Penwell Barnett, 'Intersectional harassment and deviant embodiment among autistic adults: (dis)ability, gender and sexuality' (2017) 19 *Culture, Health & Sexuality*, 1210.

[56] See, for example, Rosette et al, in note 28; Chai R. Feldblum and Victoria A. Lipnic, *Select Task Force on the Study of Harassment in the Workplace*

some contexts there may be no obvious complaint mechanism (for instance, due to lack of appropriate organizational policies) or non-disclosure agreements may apply. Disaggregated disability data may also be unavailable; even where they are, comparisons across jurisdictions are rarely straightforward due to differing definitions of disability.

Nevertheless, available international evidence indicates that disability-related harassment is widespread and pervasive, and occurs in multiple contexts globally.[57] It is clear that persons with disabilities suffer disproportionately high rates of bullying and harassment, both at work and in non-work contexts.[58] Echoing Shaw et al's findings in the US,[59] a recent study of Canadian federal public service employees found that disability was significantly associated with an increased risk of harassment.[60] In the UK, the *Fair Treatment at Work Survey*, though now dated, found that persons with a disability or long-term illness were over twice as likely to report experiencing work-related bullying or harassment,[61] and were more likely to say that they had been treated 'in a negative way' by work colleagues, clients or customers. This

---

(US Equal Employment Opportunity Commission 2016), Pt C, www.eeoc.gov/select-task-force-study-harassment-workplace (accessed 9 January 2022).

[57] Unfortunately, data on disability harassment in employment are unavailable in many jurisdictions. The sources referred to in this research are predominantly Western, though efforts have been made to cite more widely where possible.

[58] See, for example, Weber, in note 3; EHRC, in note 1.

[59] Shaw et al, in note 2.

[60] Andrea Marie Jones, Rodrigo Finkelstein and Mieke Koehoorn, 'Disability and workplace harassment and discrimination among Canadian federal public service employees' (2018) 109 *Canadian Journal of Public Health*, 79.

[61] Ralph Fevre, Theo Nichols, Gillian Prior and Ian Rutherford, *Fair Treatment at Work Report: Findings from the 2008 Survey* (Department for Business, Innovation and Skills 2009), 210–11.

included being treated in a rude or disrespectful manner (37 per cent), being the target of insults or offensive remarks (23 per cent), being humiliated or ridiculed in connection with their work (14 per cent), and being subjected to physical violence at work (9 per cent).[62] These findings are supported by the British Social Attitudes Survey (BSAS), which found that 19 per cent of people at work feel comfortable referring negatively to a person with a disability (including making jokes or using offensive language) in front of their colleagues.[63] Reviewing the findings, the EHRC highlighted 'a fairly consistent pattern', with around 20 per cent of the working population 'expressing views that acknowledge prejudice or discrimination towards disabled people'.[64] The BSAS findings are consistent with other EHRC research in the non-work context,[65] as well as with recent findings by the UK Disability Survey, which found that over half of respondents with disabilities (54 per cent) worried that they would be insulted or harassed in public places, while 45 per cent worried about being physically attacked by strangers 'at least "some of the time"'.[66] A total of 58 per cent reported being mistreated because of their disability, either online or in real life. Likewise, 42 per cent of carers were concerned that they would be insulted or harassed in public if they were with the person for whom they provided care.[67]

---

[62] Nick Coleman, Wendy Sykes and Carola Groom, *Barriers to Employment and Unfair Treatment at Work: A Quantitative Analysis of Disabled People's Experiences* (EHRC 2013), 60–1.

[63] Ibid, 60–1.

[64] Ibid, 61.

[65] EHRC, in note 1.

[66] Disability Unit, *UK Disability Survey Research Report, June 2021* (UK Government 2021), www.gov.uk/government/publications/uk-disabil ity-survey-research-report-june-2021/uk-disability-survey-research-rep ort-june-2021 (accessed 20 September 2021).

[67] Ibid.

Research on intersectional forms of harassment also highlights the prevalence of sexual harassment and violence towards women with disabilities.[68] Again, this may arise in both work and non-work settings. An EU report in 2015 identified that women with disabilities were more likely than women without disabilities to experience multiple forms of gender-based violence, including sexual harassment, in work or other contexts.[69] In the non-work context, UK data from the Office for National Statistics (ONS) showed that in the three years ending March 2018, adults with disabilities were more likely than adults without disabilities to report experiencing a sexual assault in the last year. However, women with disabilities were more than five times more likely than men with disabilities to have experienced sexual assault in the last year, and were also more likely to have experienced sexual assault than women without disabilities.[70] Recent reports on sexual harassment in the UK, Australia and Hong Kong also highlight that persons with disabilities are disproportionately affected by sexual harassment at work and other contexts.[71] Although both men

---

[68] See, for example, Devandas Aguilar, in note 52, 31–2; Buckley, in note 12.

[69] European Union Agency for Fundamental Rights, *Violence against Women: An EU-Wide Survey. Main Results* (FRA 2015), 187–9, https://fra.europa.eu/sites/default/files/fra_uploads/fra-2014-vaw-survey-main-results-apr14_en.pdf (accessed 29 October 2021).

[70] Sexual assault was defined as including attempted sexual assault. See, further, Office for National Statistics, *Disability and Crime, UK: 2019* (Office for National Statistics 2019), Pt 6, www.ons.gov.uk/peoplepopulationandcommunity/healthandsocialcare/disability/bulletins/disabilityandcrimeuk/2019 (accessed 9 January 2022). These figures subsequently fell slightly: see Office for National Statistics, 'Sexual offences victim characteristics, England and Wales: year ending March 2020' (2021), www.ons.gov.uk/peoplepopulationandcommunity/crimeandjustice/articles/sexualoffencesvictimcharacteristicsenglandandwales/march2020 (accessed 8 April 2021).

[71] Women and Equalities Committee, in note 10, 7; AHRC, in note 7, 180; James K.S. Chan, Kitty K.Y. Lam, , Christy C.M. Cheung, and Jimmy T.Y. Lo (2019) 'Break the Silence: Territory-wide Study on Sexual

and women with disabilities are at increased risk in this regard,[72] women with disabilities are more likely to experience sexual harassment than women without disabilities or men with or without disabilities.[73]

Other intersections may also the affect the prevalence of violence and harassment. Age is one; for instance, ONS data in the UK show that younger adults with disabilities were more likely to have experienced sexual assaults or attempted assaults than adults with disabilities in other age groups, and were significantly more likely to have experienced sexual assault or attempted assault than adults without disabilities in the same age group.[74] A further significant factor is (again) the type of impairment, as persons with intellectual or psychosocial disabilities are very significantly more likely to experience violence.[75] Indeed, gender and impairment type together are a particularly significant intersection with disability, as rates of sexual assault are particularly high for women who are deaf, blind or autistic, who have voice or speech impairments, or who have intellectual, psychosocial or multiple disabilities.[76]

Harassment of University Students in Hong Kong' (Hong Kong: Equal Opportunities Commission), 11.

[72] Kathleen C. Basile, Matthew J. Breiding and Sharon G. Smith, 'Disability and risk of recent sexual violence in the United States' (2016) 106 *American Journal of Public Health*, 928.

[73] Australian Institute of Health and Welfare, *People with Disability in Australia* (Australian Government 2020), www.aihw.gov.au/reports/dis ability/people-with-disability-in-australia/contents/summary (accessed 29 October 2021).

[74] Office for National Statistics (2019), in note 70, Pt 6.

[75] Grima Algora and Sen, in note 7, 5; Lan-Ping Lin and others, 'Sexual assault of people with disabilities: results of a 2002–2007 national report in Taiwan' (2009) 30 *Research in Developmental Disabilities*, 969. For similar findings in the UK, see Office for National Statistics (2019), in note 70, Pt 6. However, the ONS findings must be treated with caution, as the report advises that some of the reported disabilities may have arisen post-abuse.

[76] Devandas Aguilar, in note 52, 31–2.

1.5 Conclusion

This chapter has explored the nature of disability harassment and its interaction with harassment of other kinds. While much disability harassment derives from the othering, stigmatization and social exclusion of persons with disabilities, multiple and intersectional forms of harassment are also highly prevalent. Intersectional forms of disability harassment often arise in conjunction with gender, race, age and impairment type, among other characteristics, and may lead to synergistic harms that are specific to those intersections. Women with disabilities are particularly likely to experience sexual harassment and gender-based violence; they may also experience specific forms of sexual harassment that are not experienced by other women. Persons with psychosocial conditions are significantly more likely to experience violence, and women with particular kinds of disabilities (such as those with psychosocial or intellectual disabilities, or particular sensory impairments) are especially likely to experience sexual assault. However, persons with disabilities of all kinds experience high rates of bullying, harassment and negative treatment in work and other contexts. The evidence is therefore clear that disability harassment constitutes a serious problem, both within and outside of employment, and that the response to disability harassment must encompass intersectional forms of harassment, including sexual harassment.

TWO

The Human Rights Framework

2.1 Introduction

This chapter outlines the human rights framework for addressing disability harassment. The purpose of the chapter is to explain the legal context in which disability harassment occurs and to highlight the obligations of states to address it, particularly in the EU. The chapter begins with a brief overview of the general human rights framework relevant to both disability harassment at work and intersectional forms of discrimination. These include the International Covenant on Economic, Social and Cultural Rights (ICESCR), the Convention on the Elimination of All Forms of Discrimination against Women (CEDAW), the Convention on the Elimination of All Forms of Racial Discrimination (CERD) and regional instruments, such as the European Convention on Human Rights (ECHR) and the Protocol to the African Charter on Human and People's Rights on the Rights of Women in Africa (the Maputo Protocol). The chapter then focuses particularly on the Convention on the Rights of Persons with Disabilities (CRPD), the Framework Employment Directive (FED) in the European Union (EU)[1] and the recent ILO Violence and Harassment Convention 2019 (the ILO Convention).[2]

---

[1] Council Directive 2000/78/EC of 27 November 2000 Establishing a General Framework for Equal Treatment in Employment and Occupation [2000] OJ L 303.

[2] Violence and Harassment Convention 2019 (No. 190).

The CRPD, FED and ILO Convention were selected for closer analysis for several reasons. The CRPD has a unique status, both as the principal international instrument that addresses the human rights of persons with disabilities, and as the fastest negotiated human rights treaty in history. Its application is incredibly broad: at the time of writing, it has been ratified by 185 countries worldwide. The CRPD is also unique as the first human rights treaty capable of ratification by regional organizations; notably, it has been ratified by the EU itself, as well as by all its member states. As Buckley and Quinlivan note, the CRPD has been relied on extensively in other international contexts, including the jurisprudence of the Court of Justice of the European Union (CJEU)[3] and the European Court of Human Rights.[4] They therefore contend that 'the CRPD represents a broad consensus at European level, and that the concepts enshrined therein should guide our understanding of relevant principles and concepts'.[5]

Within the EU, the FED provides the original legal framework for addressing work-related disability harassment in member states, pre-dating the CRPD by eight years. Even in the UK, the FED remains relevant to the interpretation of the Equality Act 2010, insofar as it is not amended by

---

[3]   See, for example, Joined Cases C-335/11 and C-337/11, *HK Danmark, Acting on Behalf of Jette Ring v Dansk almennyttigt Boligselskab and HK Danmark, Acting on Behalf of Lone Skouboe Werge v Dansk Arbejdsgiverforening, Acting on Behalf of Pro Display A/S (Ring and Skouboe Werge)* [2013] ECLI:EU:C:3013: 222; Case C-363/12, *Z v A Government Department, The Board of Management of a Community School* [2014] ECLI:EU:C:2014:159.

[4]   See, for example, *Glor v Switzerland* – 13444/04 [2009] ECHR 2181 (30 April 2009); *Kiyutin v Russia* – 2700/10 [2011] ECHR 439 (10 March 2011); *Alajos Kiss v Hungary* – 38832/06 [2010] ECHR 692 (20 May 2010).

[5]   Shivaun Quinlivan and Lucy-Ann Buckley, 'Reasonable accommodation in Irish constitutional law: two steps forward and one step back – or simply out of step?' (2021) 72 *Northern Ireland Legal Quarterly*, 61, 64.

Parliament,[6] and disability discrimination law in Northern Ireland must continue to comply with EU law.[7] This chapter highlights some key differences between the CRPD and the FED which suggest that the EU has, so far, failed to fully meet its obligations under the CRPD. The chapter argues that the distinctions between the CRPD and FED are particularly important because EU member states may incorrectly assume that compliance with the FED ensures compliance with the CRPD.

The CRPD and the FED are particularly relevant to the Irish experience, explored in Chapters Four and Five, as Ireland is an EU member state and has ratified the CRPD. However, the third instrument selected for detailed discussion, the ILO Convention, has (as yet) no specific relevance to Ireland. It is included as the international instrument with the most detailed focus to date on harassment in the world of work, and because of its emphasis on multiple and intersecting forms of discrimination. This chapter therefore considers what the ILO Convention offers to the analysis of disability harassment above what is already offered by the CRPD and FED.

The chapter focuses particularly on how intersectionality informs the human rights framework. As highlighted in Chapter One, multiple and intersectional forms of harassment are central to the experience of disability discrimination. The human rights framework must therefore be capable of addressing intersectional forms of harassment if it is to combat disability harassment successfully. As Atrey puts it: 'If multiple and compounding disadvantages make a difference to the experience of human rights, as intersectionality shows that they do, there must be a broad and sustained way of connecting the

---

[6] European Union (Withdrawal Agreement) Act 2018, s 6.

[7] Agreement on the Withdrawal of the United Kingdom of Great Britain and Northern Ireland from the European Union and the European Atomic Energy Community, 2019: Protocol on Northern Ireland, Art 2(1).

discourses in intersectionality and human rights law to address such disadvantage or violation of human rights.'[8]

2.2 Locating disability harassment in the human rights framework

Harassment is not explicitly addressed in most human rights instruments.[9] However, this does not mean that disability harassment is not covered by the human rights framework. Without purporting to provide a comprehensive overview, a few key instruments may be highlighted to set the context for the subsequent discussion of the CRPD, the FED and the ILO Convention.

Of particular relevance in the employment context is the ICESCR, Article 7 of which addresses the right to 'just and favourable conditions of work'. Although Article 7 does not mention harassment specifically, it is clear that it encompasses both harassment and sexual harassment.[10] The ICESCR also prohibits discrimination in relation to the rights guaranteed under the convention and includes a non-exhaustive list of prohibited grounds of discrimination.[11] Again, although this does not explicitly reference disability, disability is included under the heading 'other status'. Outlining the scope of Article 7, General Comment No. 23 states that 'All workers should be free from physical and mental harassment, including sexual

---

[8] Shreya Atrey, 'Introduction: intersectionality from equality to human rights', in Shreya Atrey and Peter Dunne (eds), *Intersectionality and Human Rights Law* (Hart Publishing 2020), 3.

[9] Exceptions include the CRPD, the Maputo Protocol and the ILO Convention.

[10] Committee on Economic, Social and Cultural Rights (CESCR), 'General Comment No. 23 (2016) on the right to just and favourable conditions of work (Article 7 of the International Covenant on Economic, Social and Cultural Rights)' (2016) UN Doc E/C.12/GC/23 [6].

[11] ICESCR, Art 2(2).

harassment.'[12] It also highlights the need for labour legislation to define harassment broadly and with explicit reference to harassment on various grounds, including disability.[13]

At a regional level, the ECHR also does not specifically reference either harassment or disability. However, disability harassment may be encompassed as a form of discriminatory treatment under Article 14. Article 14 itself is said to be ancillary in nature, as its ambit is limited to other rights and freedoms protected under the ECHR.[14] However, while the European Court of Human Rights always examines Article 14 in conjunction with another substantive provision of the ECHR, Article 14's application is not strictly limited to that of the relevant substantive provision, and it is sufficient if the case falls within the scope, broadly speaking, of one of the other articles. Thus, Article 14 has been held to be applicable to employment,[15] even though the ECHR does not explicitly refer to either employment or the right to work.[16] Similarly, while disability is not listed in the grounds covered by Article 14, these are not exhaustive, and in practice, the European Court of Human Rights has confirmed that Article 14 includes discrimination based on disability, medical conditions or genetic features.[17] Finally, it should be noted that Protocol 12 of the ECHR confers a broader right to be free from

---

[12] CESCR, in note 10, [48].

[13] Ibid.

[14] European Court of Human Rights, 'Case relating to certain aspects of the laws on the use of languages in education in Belgium (preliminary objection and merits)' (1972) 45 *International Law Reports*, 114.

[15] See, for example, *Sidabras and Dziautas v Lithuania* – 55480/00;59330/00 [2004] ECHR 395 (27 July 2004); *Bigaeva against Greece* – 26713/05 [2011] ECHR 2164 (2 December 2011).

[16] For a detailed discussion of the scope of Article 14, see *Guide on Article 14 of the European Convention on Human Rights and on Article 1 of Protocol No. 12 to the Convention* (Council of Europe and European Court of Human Rights, 2020).

[17] *Glor v Switzerland*, in note 4; *Kiyutin v Russia*, in note 4.

discrimination in 'the enjoyment of any right set forth by law', which has also been held to encompass disability.[18] However, not all signatories to the ECHR have ratified Protocol 12.[19]

It is also clear that the international human rights framework encompasses at least some forms of multiple and intersectional discrimination of direct relevance to disability harassment. International human rights instruments have increasingly focused on specific disadvantaged groups,[20] with different instruments addressing discrimination based on race,[21] gender,[22] children[23] and disability.[24] However, de Beco notes that the new, group-specific treaties have paid particular attention to some recognized intersections (for instance, as discussed later, the CRPD focuses particularly on gender). On the other hand, disability was not explicitly considered in human rights treaties prior to the Convention on the Rights of the Child (CRC),[25] while race and ethnic origin generally remain unaddressed in treaties after the CERD.[26] To some extent, these gaps have been addressed through the work of the treaty committees. For instance, the CERD Committee has highlighted that some forms of racial discrimination have a specific gender dimension,[27] and has also highlighted

---

[18] *Negovanović and Others v Serbia* (Application No. 29907/16 and Three Others, 25 January 2022).

[19] For example, Ireland has signed but not yet ratified Protocol 12.

[20] Gauthier de Beco, 'Protecting the invisible: an intersectional approach to international human rights law' (2017) 17 *Human Rights Law Review*, 633, 636.

[21] CERD.

[22] CEDAW.

[23] Convention on the Rights of the Child (CRC).

[24] CRPD.

[25] De Beco, in note 20, 641.

[26] Race is mentioned in the Preamble of the CRPD in the context of multiple and intersectional discrimination.

[27] Committee on the Elimination of Racial Discrimination, 'General Recommendation No. 25 on Gender Related Dimensions of Racial Discrimination' (2000) UN Doc A/55/18.

intersectionality as expanding the grounds of discrimination in practice.[28] The CEDAW Committee has highlighted multiple intersections with gender[29] and adopted a recommendation on the gender dimensions of disability discrimination,[30] while the CRC Committee has adopted General Comment No. 9 on children with disabilities. The Committee on Economic, Social and Cultural Rights (CESCR) acknowledged in General Comment No. 20 that different grounds of discrimination can intersect and have a 'unique and specific impact'.[31] However, it gives only a fleeting reference to this in General Comment No. 23, noting simply that 'Intersectional discrimination and the absence of a life-cycle approach regarding the needs of women lead to accumulated disadvantages that have a negative impact on the right to just and favourable conditions of work and other rights.'[32] Other acknowledgements of intersectionality include the Beijing Declaration and Platform for Action, which recognized that women and girls 'face multiple barriers to their empowerment and advancement because of such factors as their ... disability'.[33]

---

[28] Committee on the Elimination of Racial Discrimination, 'General Recommendation No. 32, the Meaning and Scope of Special Measures in the International Convention on the Elimination of Racial Discrimination' (2009) UN Doc CERD/C/GC/32.

[29] UN Committee on the Elimination of Discrimination Against Women, 'General recommendation No. 35 on gender-based violence against women, updating general recommendation No. 19' (2017) UN Doc CEDAW/C/GC/35, [12].

[30] UN Committee on the Elimination of Discrimination Against Women, 'General Recommendation No 18 on Women with Disabilities' (1991) UN Doc A/46/38.

[31] CESCR, 'General Comment No. 20 Non-discrimination in Economic, Social and Cultural Rights (Art. 2, Para. 2 of the International Covenant on Economic, Social and Cultural Rights)' (2009) UN Doc E/C.12/GC/20, [17].

[32] CESCR, in note 10, [47(a)].

[33] UN, 'Beijing Declaration and Platform for Action, adopted at the Fourth World Conference for Women' (1995), [32].

As de Beco contends:

> the more human rights treaties deal with people sharing a number of characteristics associated with distinct marginalised groups of people, the more these people will be able to benefit from human rights protection. The greater the attention paid to them in these treaties, the less likely they are to continue to fall through the net.[34]

However, he also notes that the focus on women and children with disabilities has not been matched by a focus on other disability subgroups (for example, based on race/ethnicity).[35] It is true that the focus of the treaties has been significantly expanded in general comments and by the work of the UN special rapporteurs. Overall, however, and notwithstanding the acknowledgement by some treaty committees of intersectional concerns, de Beco contends that the protected categories in the international human rights treaties encourage a 'monolithic' understanding of identity based on the experiences of the dominant group members and tending to overlook the experiences of disadvantaged subgroups.[36] Similarly, Atrey contends that human rights theory and doctrine merely '[dabble] with intersectionality'[37] and that intersectional analysis 'needs to be centred and engaged with fundamentally in the practice of human rights law'.[38]

From a disability harassment perspective, the strongest acknowledgement of intersectional forms of harassment has related to gender. This is particularly evident in relation to the CEDAW. That convention does not refer explicitly to

---

[34] De Beco, in note 20, 641.
[35] Ibid.
[36] Ibid.
[37] Atrey, in note 8, 3.
[38] Ibid, 4.

harassment or sexual harassment. However, in a series of general recommendations, the CEDAW Committee has interpreted the prohibition of discrimination contained in the convention as encompassing gender-based violence. This is defined in General Recommendation No. 35 as 'violence which is directed against a woman because she is a woman or that affects women disproportionately'.[39] This includes acts inflicting physical, mental or sexual harm or suffering, and related threats or coercion. The CEDAW Committee has explicitly recognized that gender-based violence may also have a disability dimension.[40] More recently, the UN Special Rapporteur on Violence against Women, Its Causes and Consequences has highlighted the impact of intersectional forms of gender-based violence on marginalized groups, including women with disabilities.[41]

Regional instruments also have the potential to address intersectional forms of harassment, including disability harassment. The Maputo Protocol – to date, ratified by 42 member countries in the African Union – is unusual in explicitly affirming the right of women and girls to be free from sexual harassment, including in the workplace[42] and in education and training,[43] as well as a general right to dignity[44] and to be free from discrimination.[45] From an intersectional perspective, the Maputo Protocol requires signatories to

---

[39] CEDAW Committee, in note 29, [1].

[40] Ibid, [12].

[41] UN Human Rights Council, '15 years of the United Nations SR on Violence against Women, Its Causes and Consequences (1994–2009): a critical review' (2009) UN Doc A/HRC/11/6/Add.5, /www.unwomen. org/en/docs/2009/1/15-years-of-the-un-special-rapporteur-on-viole nce-against-women (accessed 12 November 2021).

[42] Maputo Protocol, Art 13.

[43] Ibid, Art 12.

[44] Ibid, Art 3.

[45] Ibid, Art 2.

ensure that women with disabilities are protected from violence, including sexual abuse and discrimination based on disability.[46]

The European Court of Human Rights has shown some receptiveness to intersectional approaches, albeit not in the harassment context specifically. For instance, in a case where a female complainant suffered intense pain and difficulty with sexual relations after surgery, the national court had reduced the compensation awarded, partly because it assumed that sexuality was not important for older women. The European Court of Human Rights held that this demonstrated particular prejudices on the part of the national judiciary.[47] However, the court has been unreceptive to claims of intersectional discrimination by Muslim women (for instance, in relation to so-called 'headscarf bans'),[48] and there is evidence that this intersectional group of complainants is least successful in litigation before the court.[49] The court has also avoided addressing Article 14 in several cases involving the non-consensual sterilization of Roma women, instead finding for the complainants under other articles of the convention.[50]

From a disability perspective, the most important human rights instrument is undoubtedly the CRPD, adopted in 2008. The CRPD references harassment only briefly, in relation to

---

[46] Ibid, Art 23.

[47] *Carvalho Pinto de Sousa v Portugal* – 17484/15 [2017] ECHR 719 (25 July 2017).

[48] See, for example, *SAS v France* [2014] ECHR 695.

[49] Pablo Castillo-Ortiz, Amal Ali and Navajyoti Samanta, 'Gender, intersectionality, and religious manifestation before the European Court of Human Rights' (2019) 18 Journal of Human Rights 76.

[50] For example, *N.B. v Slovakia* – 29518/10 [2012] ECHR 991 (12 June 2012); *V.C. v Slovakia* – 18968/07 [2011] ECHR 1888 (8 November 2011). See, further, Siobhan Curran, 'Intersectionality and human rights law: an examination of the coercive sterilisations of Romani Women' (2016) 16 *Equal Rights Review*, 132.

employment.[51] However, its prohibition on discrimination, which applies across contexts, has also been interpreted as encompassing harassment.[52] The CRPD explicitly references intersectional forms of discrimination, which would also apply to harassment. The CRPD is considered in detail in Section 2.3.

A more explicit approach is taken by the ILO Convention. Like the CRPD, this convention is particularly significant for its explicit focus on intersectionality, including on the disability ground. This is considered in detail in Section 2.6.

Finally, the provisions of EU law must be considered as particularly relevant to the employment law context addressed in this book. Although not a human rights treaty, the FED is of major importance in addressing disability harassment in employment in EU member states. However, although the EU's legal framework addresses harassment based on gender, disability, race and other grounds, it does not yet address intersectional forms of harassment. Again, this is considered in detail in Section 2.4.

2.3 The Convention on the Rights of Persons with Disabilities

The CRPD is commonly said to adopt a social model of disability, meaning that difficulties experienced by persons with disabilities are considered to derive from exclusionary social structures, attitudes and practices. This contrasts with the medical model of disability, where difficulties are seen as deriving from a person's impairment, rather than structural or

---

[51] CRPD, Art 27(1)(b).

[52] UN Committee on the Rights of Persons with Disabilities (CRPD Committee), 'General Comment No. 6 (2018) on Equality and Non-discrimination' (2018) UN Doc CRPD/C/GC/6, [18(d)].

social causes.[53] Disability itself is not defined in the CRPD, and the Preamble to the convention acknowledges that it is an 'evolving concept'.[54] However, Article 1, addressing the purpose of the convention, states that 'Persons with disabilities include those who have long-term physical, mental, intellectual or sensory impairments which in interaction with various barriers may hinder their full and effective participation in society on an equal basis with others.' The language of Article 1 clearly indicates that it is not intended to be an exhaustive definition, but rather inclusive and indicative. Notably, the CRPD does not require that a disability must affect an individual's ability to function, either in work or in other contexts. Indeed, the Preamble notes that barriers to participation may be 'attitudinal and environmental',[55] suggesting that they may result purely from social prejudice, stigma or stereotyping.

In terms of addressing harassment, Article 5 requires states parties to, among other things, 'prohibit all discrimination on the basis of disability and guarantee to persons with disabilities equal and effective legal protection against discrimination on all grounds'.[56] The obligation to prohibit discrimination and promote equality under Article 5 is immediately realizable[57] and applies to private and public enterprises.[58] The CRPD Committee has identified four main forms of discrimination covered by Article 5: direct discrimination; indirect discrimination; the denial of reasonable accommodation; and harassment.[59] The CRPD Committee further states:

---

[53] See, further, Quinlivan and Buckley, in note 5, 68.

[54] CRPD, Preamble, [e].

[55] Ibid.

[56] CRPD, Art 5(2).

[57] CRPD Committee, in note 52, [12].

[58] CRPD, Art 4(1)(e).

[59] Ibid, [18].

'Harassment' is a form of discrimination when unwanted conduct related to disability or other prohibited grounds takes place with the purpose or effect of violating the dignity of a person and of creating an intimidating, hostile, degrading, humiliating or offensive environment. It can happen through actions or words that have the effect of perpetuating the difference and oppression of persons with disabilities.[60]

Disability harassment is also captured in Article 16 of the CRPD, which requires states 'to protect persons with disabilities, both within and outside the home, from all forms of exploitation, violence and abuse, including their gender-based aspects'.[61] Clearly, the scope of Article 16 is broader than harassment and may include hate crimes and gender-based violence, among other forms of abuse.

Article 27 specifically references harassment in employment. This requires states to 'Protect the rights of persons with disabilities, on an equal basis with others, to just and favourable conditions of work, including ... safe and healthy working conditions, including protection from harassment, and the redress of grievances'.[62]

The CRPD Committee recently published a 'Draft general comment on Article 27',[63] which reiterates the understanding of harassment outlined in General Comment No. 6. However, the draft general comment also refers to the definition of harassment in the ILO Convention (discussed

---

[60] Ibid, [18(d)].

[61] CRPD, Art 16(1).

[62] Ibid, Art 27(b).

[63] CRPD Committee, 'Draft general comment on Article 27 on the right of persons with disabilities to work and employment', www.ohchr.org/EN/HRBodies/CRPD/Pages/GeneralDiscussions.aspx (accessed 11 January 2022 but since removed).

in Section 2.6),[64] suggesting that CRPD jurisprudence is likely to be influenced further by that convention. It also cites a range of examples taken from the Australian Human Rights Commission (AHRC), as follows: 'Harassment in the workplace can include excluding or isolating employees, psychological harassment, intimidation, assigning meaningless tasks unrelated to the job, giving employees impossible jobs, deliberately changed work rosters to inconvenience particular employees, undermining work performance by deliberately withholding information vital for effective work performance.'[65] What is most striking about these examples is that they are generic rather than disability specific. This suggests that under the CRPD, the reason for harassment is more important than the form it takes.

The CRPD consistently emphasizes the importance of an intersectional approach in identifying and addressing discrimination. From the outset, it expresses concern regarding the 'difficult conditions faced by persons with disabilities who are subject to multiple or aggravated forms of discrimination on the basis of race, colour, sex, language, religion, political or other opinion, national, ethnic, indigenous or social origin, property, birth, age or other status'.[66] In Article 6, it emphasizes the need for a gender perspective and recognizes that women and girls with disabilities are at greater risk of violence, abuse, neglect and exploitation.[67] The CRPD Committee has likewise repeatedly highlighted not only the intersection of gender and disability, as well as the scale of violence against women with disabilities, but also the importance of further intersections, including those based on sexual orientation, race, ethnicity, age and religion, or those based

---

[64] Ibid, [23].

[65] AHRC, 'Workplace discrimination harassment and bullying' (AHRC 2014), cited in CRPD Committee, in note 63, [23].

[66] CRPD, Preamble, [16].

[67] Ibid, [17].

on particular kinds of disability.[68] The CRPD Committee has also distinguished between multiple and intersectional discrimination, emphasizing that multiple discrimination refers to 'a situation where a person can experience discrimination on two or several grounds, in the sense that discrimination is compounded or aggravated', while intersectional discrimination 'refers to a situation where several grounds operate and interact with each other at the same time in such a way that they are inseparable and thereby expose relevant individuals to unique types of disadvantage and discrimination'.[69] In its draft general comment on Article 27, the CRPD Committee notes that 'Intersectional discrimination recognizes that individuals do not experience discrimination as members of a homogenous group but, rather, as individuals with multidimensional layers of identities, statuses and life circumstances'.[70]

As cross-cutting articles, Articles 5 and 6 must be applied in interpreting other provisions of the convention. In the context of Article 27 (work and employment), states must expressly prohibit work-related discrimination, including harassment and intersectional discrimination,[71] as well as victimization (retaliation).[72] The CRPD Committee has further emphasized that such legislative measures must be premised on a broad and inclusive definition of disability, which 'seeks to outlaw and prevent a discriminatory act rather than target a defined protected group' and does not place the burden on complainants to prove that they are 'disabled enough' to merit legal protection.[73] The

---

[68] See, for example, CRPD Committee, in note 52, [19], [21]; CRPD Committee, 'General Comment No. 3 (2016), Article 6: Women and Girls with Disabilities' (2016) UN Doc CRPD/C/GC/3, [5].

[69] CRPD Committee, 'General Comment No. 6 (2018) on equality and non-discrimination on Article 5' (2018) UN Doc CRPD/C/GC/6, [19].

[70] CRPD Committee, in note 63, [24].

[71] CRPD Committee, in note 52, [67(d)].

[72] Ibid, [73(i)].

[73] Ibid, [73(b)].

definition of disability should therefore include past, present, future and imputed (perceived) disabilities, as well as persons associated with persons with disabilities.[74] Furthermore, the requirement in Article 5 to prohibit 'discrimination on all grounds' 'means that all possible grounds of discrimination and their intersections must be taken into account'.[75] Procedural rules shifting the burden of proof in civil cases where the facts raise a presumption of discrimination are also required.[76] Anti-discrimination legislation must include 'appropriate and effective legal remedies and sanctions', including systemic remedies and financial compensation.[77] Sanctions for the breach of the right to equality must be '[e]ffective, proportionate and dissuasive'.[78]

Finally, the CRPD Committee has highlighted that states' obligations do not end with the enactment of legislation, but include the duty to monitor discrimination claims, both adjudicated and settled, and to collect disaggregated data on outcomes and sanctions.[79] States must also '[e]stablish accessible and effective redress mechanisms and ensure access to justice, on an equal basis with others, for victims of discrimination based on disability'.[80] This may require access to affordable legal aid, where necessary.[81]

2.4 European Union law and the Framework Employment Directive

Employment-related disability harassment is prohibited in EU law under the FED, which addresses discrimination based

---

[74] Ibid, [73(b)], [20].

[75] Ibid, [21].

[76] Ibid, [73(i)].

[77] Ibid, [22].

[78] Ibid, [31(f)].

[79] Ibid, [73(g)], [34].

[80] Ibid, [73(h)].

[81] Ibid, [73(h)].

on disability, sexual orientation, age and religion or belief. Although pre-dating the CRPD, the provisions of the FED satisfy many of the CRPD's requirements, addressing direct and indirect discrimination, reasonable accommodation, harassment, victimization, and the burden of proof, among other considerations. It also appears to encompass discrimination by association,[82] though it is not yet clear if it includes discrimination based on perceived characteristics.[83] Like the CRPD, remedies under the FED should be 'effective, proportionate and dissuasive'.[84] The CJEU has issued detailed guidance on what this means in practice,[85] but a recent report notes that some national courts tend to make relatively low awards, which can discourage victims from taking legal action or seeking financial compensation as a remedy.[86] The FED does not explicitly require the collection of equality data, falling short of the CRPD in this respect, but the EU is nevertheless obliged to report periodically to the CRPD Committee on the progress of implementation and compliance.

Compared with UN treaties, the FED is unusually explicit on disability harassment. As Article 2(3) states:

Harassment shall be deemed to be a form of discrimination ... when unwanted conduct related to any

---

[82] Case C-306/06, *Coleman v Attridge Law* [2008] ECR I-5603; Case C-83/14, *CHEZ Razpredelenie Bulgaria*, ECLI:EU:C:2015:480.

[83] The court did not take the opportunity to address this in Case C-354/13, *FOA Acting on Behalf of Karsten Kaltoft* [2014] ECLI:EU:C:2014:2463.

[84] FED, Art 17 and Recital 35.

[85] For a summary, see European Commission, 'Report on the application of Council Directive 2000/43/EC implementing the principle of equal treatment between persons irrespective of racial or ethnic origin ("the Racial Equality Directive") and of Council Directive 2000/78/EC establishing a general framework for equal treatment in employment and occupation ("the Employment Equality Directive")' (Com No 139 final, 2021), [2.2.4].

[86] Ibid.

of the grounds ... takes place with the purpose or effect of violating the dignity of a person and of creating an intimidating, hostile, degrading, humiliating or offensive environment. In this context, the concept of harassment may be defined in accordance with the national laws and practice of the Member States.

The FED states that the definition of harassment is a matter for national law.[87] However, it appears that it includes harassment based on the victim's association with someone who is disabled. In *Coleman*, the CJEU held that harassment of the plaintiff in connection with her child's disability would constitute unlawful discrimination. The court considered that ruling otherwise would undermine the effectiveness of the FED and deprive persons with disabilities of an important element of protection.[88] Although it has been suggested that the FED's requirements in relation to the burden of proof do not apply to harassment,[89] this does not appear to be the case, as the CJEU was adamant in *Coleman* that the same rules applied to harassment as to other forms of discrimination.[90] The European Commission has, however, noted that there may be some inconsistencies in the application of the correct rules on the burden of proof.[91]

The language of the FED regarding harassment is identical to that later adopted by the CRPD Committee in its General Comment No. 6 (outlined previously). This is perhaps unsurprising, as the EU took a leading role in negotiating the

---

[87] FED, Art 2(3).

[88] *Coleman*, in note 82, [51].

[89] Lisa Waddington and Andrea Broderick (2019) 'Combatting disability discrimination and realising equality: a comparison of the UN CRPD and EU equality and non-discrimination law', European Commission, 84, https://data.europa.eu/doi/10.2838/478746 (accessed 12 January 2022).

[90] *Coleman*, in note 82, [61].

[91] European Commission, in note 85, [2.2.2].

CRPD.[92] Nevertheless, the similarity of phrasing clearly indicates that the conceptualization in the FED is compliant with the CRPD.

The FED does however fall short of CRPD requirements in some significant respects. The scope of the FED is much narrower than the CRPD, addressing only employment and vocational training. This is because the EU is limited in its legislative competence. It must therefore be highlighted that combatting disability discrimination is an area of shared competence, meaning that both the EU and its member states have the power to act in this area. As all EU member states have independently ratified the CRPD, all bear individual responsibility for compliance, irrespective of the EU's duty.

Scope apart, however, two key issues arise. The first derives from the FED's failure to define what is meant by 'disability'. This initially resulted in the CJEU taking a medical approach and requiring complainants to demonstrate a limitation arising from an impairment.[93] In *Chacon Navas*, the CJEU emphasized that a disability, within the meaning of the FED, 'must be understood as referring to a limitation that results in particular from physical, mental or psychological impairments and that hinders the participation of the person concerned in professional life'.[94] The CJEU clearly considered that the barrier to participation must arise from the impairment, precluding an examination of the impact of social structures. As discussed in Section 2.5, this has since been partly addressed, but some outstanding concerns remain.

The second issue relates to the failure of the FED to address intersectional discrimination. EU law prohibits discrimination on a range of grounds, though different levels of protection

---

[92] Waddington and Broderick, in note 89, 31.

[93] Case C-13/05, *Chacón Navas v Eurest Colectividades SA* [2006] ECLI:EU:C:2006:456.

[94] Ibid, [43].

apply to each, leading to what has been termed a 'hierarchy of discrimination grounds'.[95] Thus, racial harassment must be addressed in both employment and various non-employment contexts, such as education and healthcare. However, the scope of protection in relation to gender is narrower, and protection in relation to disability is narrower still, being limited to employment and vocational training. These differences present significant practical difficulties to applying an intersectional approach to discrimination law.[96]

Even so, it has been argued that current EU law permits an intersectional approach.[97] The European Commission stated in 2014 that the equality Directives already covered the combined effect of two or more discriminatory grounds.[98] Schiek offers a detailed analysis of recognition of multiple discrimination in various sources of EU law.[99] Likewise, in a report on intersectional discrimination in EU law, Fredman argues that CJEU jurisprudence had implicitly accepted the concept of intersectionality in at least some cases by adopting a 'capacious' interpretation of individual discriminatory grounds – that is, it was willing to consider nuances within an individual ground by considering the effect of different power relationships to create specific kinds of disadvantages.[100] Recital 3 of the FED explicitly acknowledges the impact of multiple

---

[95] Mark Bell and Lisa Waddington, 'Reflecting on inequalities in European equality law' (2003) 28 *European Law Review*, 349, 350.

[96] Lucy-Ann Buckley, 'Women with disabilities: forever on the edge of #MeToo?', in Ann M. Noel and David B. Oppenheimer (eds), *The Globalization of the #MeToo Movement* (Fastcase and Full Court Press 2020), 419, 423.

[97] Dagmar Schiek, 'On uses, mis-uses and non-uses of intersectionality before the Court of Justice (EU)' (2018) 18 *International Journal of Discrimination and the Law*, 82.

[98] European Commission, in note 85, [4.4].

[99] Schiek, in note 97.

[100] Directorate-General for Justice and Consumers (European Commission), European Network of Legal Experts in Gender Equality and

discrimination on women, suggesting that an intersectional approach is appropriate in the gender context, at least,[101] while the potential intersection of barriers based on age and sex is acknowledged in Article 6. Atrey notes that the broad definitions of direct and indirect discrimination in the FED, combined with Recital 3, additionally support the case for an intersectional interpretation.[102]

However, in *Parris v TCD*,[103] the CJEU held that the FED does not encompass intersectional disadvantage based on multiple characteristics (in that case, sexual orientation and age). Recognizing that discrimination might be based on several grounds, the CJEU nevertheless held that a new category of discrimination could not arise unless discrimination on an individual relevant ground had been established. This completely undermines the basis for intersectional claims, as, by definition, some harms may arise due to the combined effect of different characteristics, rather than within the categories themselves.[104] The court has likewise ignored the intersectional impact of 'headscarf' bans, viewing the matter through a religious equality lens only (with extensive justifications

Non-discrimination and Sandra Fredman, *Intersectional Discrimination in EU Gender Equality and Non-discrimination Law* (Publications Office of the European Union 2016), 8.

[101] While 'multiple discrimination' is differentiated from 'intersectional discrimination' by the CRPD Committee, it has been noted that the term 'multiple discrimination' appears to be used as an 'overarching notion' at the EU level. Suzanne Burri and Dagmar Schiek, *Multiple Discrimination in EU Law: Opportunities for Legal Responses to Intersectional Gender Discrimination?* (European Commission 2009), 1, 4.

[102] Shreya Atrey, 'Illuminating the CJEU's blind spot of intersectional discrimination in *Parris v Trinity College Dublin*' (2018) 47 *Industrial Law Journal*, 278, 285–6.

[103] Case C-443/15, *David L Parris v Trinity College Dublin and others* [2016] ECLI:EU:C:2016:897.

[104] For a detailed analysis, see Atrey, in note 102; Schiek, in note 97.

permitted in respect of religious discrimination), rather than as arguably a combined impact based on gender and race.[105]

A 'capacious' approach might yet be taken to the interpretation of individual grounds, though such an approach was also not evident in *Parris*[106] or indeed the 'headscarf' cases, *Achbita*[107] and *Bougnaoui*.[108] A capacious approach would be particularly appropriate to disability given the requirement to interpret the FED as far as possible in compliance with the CRPD (discussed in Section 2.5). However, Fredman notes that the case law in this regard is mixed.[109] Combined with the ruling in *Parris*, it seems clear that, at present, there is little scope for a more expansive, intersectional approach at the EU level. This leads to a continuing shortfall in CRPD compliance.

2.5 Interaction of the CRPD and the FED

Following EU ratification of the CRPD, the CJEU has emphasized that EU law must be interpreted as consistently as possible with the CRPD.[110] This has led to an interpretation of disability more aligned with the social understanding enshrined in the CRPD. In *Ring and Werge*, the CJEU stated that a disability:

> must be understood as referring to a limitation which results in particular from physical, mental or psychological impairments which in interaction with various barriers

---

[105] Schiek, in note 97.

[106] Atrey, in note 102, 294.

[107] *Samira Achbita and Centrum voor Gelijkheid van Kansen en voor Racismebestrijding v G4S Secure Solutions NV* [2016] ECLI:C:2016:382 [2017] ECLI:EU:C:2017:203.

[108] C–188/15, *Asma Bougnaoui and Association de Défense des Droits de l'Homme (ADDH) v Micropole SA* [2017] ECLI:EU:C:2017:204.

[109] Fredman, in note 100, 11.

[110] *Ring and Werge*, in note 3.

may hinder the full and effective participation of the person concerned in professional life on an equal basis with other workers, and the limitation is a long-term one.[111]

However, while the recognition of the interaction between the impairment and social structures and barriers moves the definition more towards the social model of disability, the CJEU's approach still falls short of full CRPD compliance.

First, the CJEU's emphasis on the need for a 'limitation' suggests that impairments with a purely prejudicial effect (such as facial scarring or asymptomatic conditions) may not be covered by the FED. As noted previously, the CRPD does not make reference to a 'limitation' of the ability to function, but rather to the interaction of an impairment and 'various barriers', including attitudinal barriers. In their detailed analysis of the compliance of the FED with the CRPD, Waddington and Broderick identify concerns regarding the degree to which the CJEU is willing to recognize purely social barriers and point to cases such as *Kaltoft*, where the court gave examples of physical barriers only (though it did not explicitly state that only physical barriers would suffice).[112] They conclude:

> In essence, it seems that individuals who are 'disabled' by the false assumptions and prejudice of others about their ability – by discrimination – but who do not experience a physical or mental limitation linked to their impairment, may be excluded from protection from disability discrimination under the Court's definition of disability.[113]

Second, the definition in *Ring and Werge* emphasized that the impairment must be long-term, whereas Article 1 of the

---

[111] Ibid, [93].

[112] *Kaltoft*, in note 83, [60].

[113] Waddington and Broderick, in note 89, 58.

CRPD states that disability 'includes' impairments that are long-term.[114] The CJEU subsequently held that a condition or illness may also come within the scope of the FED where the prognosis is uncertain and the condition is therefore potentially long-lasting.[115] However, this ameliorates the requirement rather than removing it. Waddington and Broderick note that the CJEU failed to indicate a required duration for a condition to qualify as 'long-term'[116] and that medical evidence may be significantly more problematic than the court apparently assumed.[117]

Third, the CJEU's emphasis on a condition that interacts with barriers to hinder participation 'in professional life' is far narrower than Article 1 of the CRPD, which refers to 'participation in society on an equal basis with others' and is not restricted to a particular area of life. However, even if the restriction to professional life were accepted as a necessary limitation of the scope of the FED, its application by the CJEU seems unnecessarily restrictive. For example, in *Z v A Government Department*,[118] the complainant's lack of a uterus meant that she had to avail of a surrogacy arrangement to have a child. As she had not given birth, she was unable to avail of maternity leave under Irish law. However, because she was registered as the birth mother under Californian surrogacy law, she was also unable to avail of adoptive leave, meaning that no paid form of parenting leave was available to her. The CJEU held that an inability to have children by conventional

---

[114] This appears to be a misinterpretation of Article 1(2) of the CRPD, as the CJEU stated that 'it follows from the second paragraph of Article 1 of the UN Convention that the physical, mental or psychological impairments must be "long-term"': *Ring and Werge*, in note 3 [39].

[115] C-395/15, *Mohamed Daouidi v Bootes Plus SL, Fondo de Garantía Salarial, Ministerio Fiscal* [2016] ECLI:EU:C:2016:917.

[116] Waddington and Broderick, in note 89, 60.

[117] Ibid, 62.

[118] *Z*, in note 3.

means did not hinder the plaintiff's ability to participate in professional life. Hence, she did not have a disability within the meaning of the FED. However, as Buckley has noted, the lack of a paid leave entitlement meant that the plaintiff was unable to participate in professional life *on an equal basis with others*.[119] By construing the plaintiff's disability as simply the inability to bear children and holding that this, 'by itself',[120] did not hinder her ability to engage or advance in employment, the CJEU overlooked the impact of structural barriers (the rules for paid leave) on the plaintiff's ability to participate on equal terms to persons without a similar impairment. Arguably, the CJEU failed to apply even its own definition in *Ring and Werge*, which referred to a limitation resulting from the interaction of an impairment and various barriers. That definition was cited by the CJEU, but the court's application seems to have focused on the impairment alone. In other words, the CJEU cited a more social understanding of disability but, in practice, applied a medical model.[121]

The understanding of disability in the FED is important because a restrictive model of disability necessarily limits the ambit of protection from harassment and other forms of discrimination. For example, if someone were to be harassed in relation to a condition that did not in itself affect their ability to work – for instance, if the plaintiff in *Z* received upsetting comments in relation to her inability to bear children – the

---

[119] Lucy-Ann Buckley, ' "Doing gender" and Irish employment law', in Lynsey Black and Peter Dunne (eds), *Gender in Ireland: Law, Reform, Critique* (Hart Publishing 2019), 242.

[120] *Z*, in note 3 [81].

[121] The same criticism may be applied to the opinion of Advocate General Wahl of 26 September 2013 in *Z*, in note 3. Advocate General Wahl discusses the social model in some detail (at [85]) and emphasizes the interaction of the impairment with barriers ([95–6]) but then considers the limitation only in terms of whether the inability to bear children impacted on the participation in employment ([97]).

CJEU's current interpretation of disability suggests that she would potentially have no remedy under the FED.[122] It remains to be seen if the CJEU would adopt a more expansive approach in such a situation, either on the basis of a perception of disability or because it is, after all, willing to recognize attitudinal barriers.

The decision in *Z* also demonstrates the implications of a failure to take an intersectional approach. Ms Z was deprived of maternity leave because of a disability (the lack of a uterus) that primarily affects women[123] and that resulted in an inability to give birth as other women do. As Buckley notes, Ms Z was therefore 'denied the opportunity to reconcile family life and labour market participation on an equal basis with other mothers',[124] a deprivation that must be understood 'in the broader context of gendered care roles and expectations'.[125] It follows that had she been harassed on this basis, that harassment would also have been intersectional in nature, and construing it as simply gender based or disability based would have failed to capture the full nature of the harm experienced.

Although the CJEU in *Z* confirmed that the FED must be interpreted as far as possible in compliance with the CRPD and referenced Article 6 CRPD in full, neither it nor the opinion of Advocate General Wahl referenced the issue of intersectionality or the 'combined effect' of different grounds, as it was later referred to in *Parris*. This was surprising, as intersectional discrimination was apparently referenced during the oral proceedings.[126] This raises the interesting question of what

---

[122] Unless the comments could be construed as gender related, in which case, they might constitute sex discrimination.

[123] Transgender men and intersex, non-binary and gender-non-conforming persons may also be affected.

[124] Buckley, in note 119, 242.

[125] Ibid, 243.

[126] Raphaele Xenidis, 'Multiple discrimination in EU anti-discrimination law: towards redressing complex inequality?', in Uladzislau Belavusau and Kristin Henrard (eds), *EU Anti-discrimination Law beyond Gender* (Hart

would happen if an intersectional discrimination claim related to disability were explicitly framed with reference to the EU's CRPD obligations: would the CJEU revisit *Parris*, as it revisited *Chacon Navas*? It is difficult to see how the CJEU's categorical rejection of combined discrimination could be reformulated to permit intersectional claims based on disability, and indeed such a limited acceptance of intersectionality would arguably not comply with the CRPD given the emphasis in Article 5(2) on the need to protect persons with disabilities against 'discrimination on all grounds'. This point receives additional emphasis in General Comment No. 6, where the CRPD Committee states that 'Protection against "discrimination on all grounds" means that all possible grounds of discrimination and their intersections must be taken into account.'[127] It must also be noted that in its concluding observations to the EU, the CRPD Committee specifically recommended that the EU should address multiple and intersectional discrimination.[128] Multiple discrimination (including discrimination based on combinations of protected grounds) is currently referenced in a proposed new equality directive, which has not been adopted, however, despite being under discussion since 2008.[129] However, the recent adoption by the European Parliament of a resolution on intersectional discrimination, focusing particularly on gender and race but also mentioning disability and other characteristics, may provide an impetus for change.[130]

Publishing 2018), 28, www.research.ed.ac.uk/en/publications/multi ple-discrimination-in-eu-anti-discrimination-law-towards-red (accessed 5 May 2022).

[127] CRPD Committee, in note 52, [21].

[128] CRPD Committee, 'Concluding observations on the initial report of the European Union' (2015) UN Doc CRPD/C/EU/CO/1, [19].

[129] Waddington and Broderick, in note 89, 69.

[130] European Parliament resolution of 6 July 2022 on intersectional discrimination in the European Union: the socio-economic situation of women of African, Middle-Eastern, Latin-American and Asian descent (2021/2243 (INI)).

2.6 The International Labour Organization Convention

The most recent measure to address harassment at work is the ILO Convention, which entered into force on 25 June 2021. The convention is supplemented by Recommendation No. 206, which provides detailed (though non-binding) guidance on the convention's application. Although ratified by only 19 countries at the time of writing, the convention is highly significant as it heralds a new approach to workplace harassment and violence. While the convention has many novel aspects, the following may be highlighted as directly relevant to disability harassment.

First, the convention recharacterizes harassment not just as a form of discrimination, but also as a breach of a universal right to a safe and respectful working environment. This recharacterization builds on the right in Article 7 of the ICESCR to 'just and favourable conditions of work', as interpreted by the CESCR in its General Comment No. 23.[131] This is evident in the Preamble to the ILO Convention, which explicitly recognizes 'the right of everyone to a world of work free from violence and harassment, including gender-based violence and harassment'. The Preamble also notes that 'violence and harassment in the world of work can constitute a human rights violation or abuse', as well as being 'a threat to equal opportunities'. For this reason, the ILO Convention applies to all workers 'and other persons in the world of work', irrespective of employment status,[132] whether in the public or private sector, or in the formal or informal economy.[133] It applies beyond the workplace to other work-related spaces and contexts, such as while commuting, during work trips and

---

[131] CESCR, in note 10; on harassment, see [48–9].

[132] ILO Convention, Art 2. Similarly, Art 7 of the ICESCR applies to 'all workers in all settings', though no reference is made in General Comment No. 23 to such situations as commuting. See CESCR, in note 10, [5].

[133] ILO Convention, Art 2.

training, in relation to rest facilities, and in 'public and private spaces where they are a place of work'.[134] It also applies in work-related communications, including those made through communication technologies,[135] such as email and social media. Conceptualizing freedom from work-related violence and harassment as a general human right does not mean that the ILO Convention ignores the equality aspects of violence and harassment; rather, it explicitly references equality and notes that some groups 'are disproportionately affected by violence and harassment in the world of work'.[136] This would clearly include persons with disabilities. The accompanying Recommendation No. 206 also emphasizes that states should address work-related violence and harassment in multiple contexts, including occupational health and safety, equality and non-discrimination law, and criminal law.[137]

Second, the ILO Convention explicitly recognizes the multifaceted harms that may result from work-related violence and harassment. The Preamble notes that harassment 'affects a person's psychological, physical and sexual health, dignity, and family and social environment', and that it may have additional consequences, such as preventing people 'from accessing, and remaining and advancing in the labour market'. While the Preamble particularly references women in this regard, harassment may also have an excluding or limiting effect on the employment of persons with disabilities.

Third, the ILO Convention provides a single, unified and extensive concept of violence and harassment, allowing scope to address both disability hate crime and harassment. Although leaving it open to states to define violence and harassment as a single or two separate concepts, Article 1 states:

---

[134] Ibid, Art 3.

[135] Ibid, Art 3.

[136] Ibid, Art 6.

[137] ILO, 'Violence and harassment recommendation' (2019) (Recommendation No. 206), [2].

the term 'violence and harassment' in the world of work refers to a range of unacceptable behaviours and practices, or threats thereof, whether a single occurrence or repeated, that aim at, result in, or are likely to result in physical, psychological, sexual or economic harm, and includes gender-based violence and harassment.

The definition is expansive, rather than prescriptive, and focuses on actual or potential harm, rather than the nature of the conduct. Indeed, the only requirement in relation to the form of the conduct is that it must be 'unacceptable'. It appears that this is to be assessed both subjectively and objectively,[138] that is, the conduct must be unacceptable both to the victim and to a reasonable person. The definition also clarifies that a single incident may suffice, provided it is 'unacceptable' and causes or is likely to cause harm. Again, 'harm' is broadly defined and includes economic harm, such as the loss of income or employment benefits, career opportunities, or access to the labour market. The definition does not require intent or awareness by the perpetrator, either in relation to the acceptability of the conduct or the potential for harm. It is sufficient that the behaviour is unacceptable and that harm is caused or likely to result. Finally, the convention notes that violence and harassment by third parties should also be addressed.[139]

Fourth, the ILO Convention explicitly recognizes both the impact of 'multiple and intersecting forms of discrimination',[140] and the need to protect workers from 'one or more vulnerable

---

[138] International Labour Office, *Violence and Harassment in the World of Work; a Guide on Convention No. 190 and Recommendation No. 206* (International Labour Office 2021), 8, www.ilo.org/global/topics/violence-harassm ent/resources/WCMS_814507/lang--en/index.htm (accessed 12 January 2022).

[139] ILO Convention, Art 4(2).

[140] Ibid, Preamble.

groups' or 'groups in situations of vulnerability'.[141] Rather than listing examples of particular intersecting characteristics, the Convention leaves it open and maintains flexibility. The non-binding Recommendation No. 206 then states that groups meriting particular attention should be interpreted by reference to international labour standards and human rights instruments (the CRPD, with other instruments, is mentioned in the Preamble).[142] However, the convention also addresses intersectional concerns in other ways as a recurring theme. The Preamble highlights the impact of gender-based violence and harassment on women, though the definition of gender-based violence in Article 4 is notably not restricted to women. The Preamble also refers to the impact of 'gender stereotypes' and 'unequal gender-based power relations', which may be 'underlying causes' of violence and harassment. Both the ILO Convention and Recommendation No. 206 make frequent references to gender-based violence, the impact on women workers and the need for a 'gender-responsive' approach.[143] Recommendation No. 206 also references the need to protect migrant workers, particularly those who are women.[144] While the primary focus is on gender, there are also references to disability. The convention specifically references accessibility as a core principle, both in relation to information, awareness raising and training, and in relation to prevention and enforcement processes,[145] while Recommendation No. 206 notes the need to 'take into account factors that increase the likelihood of violence and harassment, including psychosocial hazards and risks'.[146] Like

---

[141] Ibid, Art 6.

[142] ILO, in note 136, [13].

[143] For example, ILO Convention, Preamble and Arts 6, 7, 9 and 10; ILO, in note 136, [12], [16].

[144] ILO, in note 136, [10].

[145] ILO Convention, Art 9(d).

[146] ILO, in note 136, [8], [20].

the CRPD, Recommendation No. 206 particularly emphasizes the need for disaggregated data.[147]

Fifth, the ILO Convention places detailed and specific positive duties on states to address violence and harassment in the world of work. These include duties in relation to monitoring, policy formation, enforcement mechanisms, remedies and support for victims, awareness raising and education, and effective inspection and investigation.[148] The convention takes a holistic view of the different aspects of prevention and redress, recognizing the complementary roles of individuals and bodies. As a labour convention, it advocates a sectoral approach where necessary and refers explicitly to the informal economy.[149] The duty to legislate is detailed and specific, and includes the duty to consult with workers when developing workplace policies.[150] Notably, and in keeping with the focus on health and safety, the convention requires states to ensure that workers 'have the right to remove themselves from a work situation which they have reasonable justification to believe presents an imminent and serious danger to life, health or safety due to violence and harassment, without suffering retaliation or other undue consequences'.[151] States must also protect workers from victimization for making complaints or whistle-blowing.[152]

Finally, and uniquely, Recommendation No. 206 advises that 'Perpetrators of violence and harassment in the world of work should be held accountable and provided counselling or other measures, where appropriate, with a view to preventing

---

[147] Ibid, [22].
[148] ILO Convention, Art 4. Many of these duties are also to be found in CESCR, in note 10.
[149] ILO Convention, Art 8.
[150] Ibid, Art 9.
[151] Ibid, Art 10(8).
[152] Ibid, Art 10.

the reoccurrence of violence and harassment, and facilitating their reintegration into work, where appropriate.'[153]

It is interesting to contrast the approaches of the CRPD, the FED and the ILO Convention. The CRPD and the FED conceptualize disability harassment specifically as a form of disability discrimination, which it undoubtedly is. The ILO Convention goes further, identifying work-related violence and harassment as a human rights abuse, in much more detail than the ICESCR, irrespective of whether it also amounts to discrimination. In this regard, the ILO Convention walks a delicate line, recognizing both a general right to freedom from harassment, while simultaneously emphasizing that harassment has particular equality implications. One consequence of this is that the ILO Convention mandates a multi-pronged approach, requiring states to address work-related harassment through a range of legislative means (anti-discrimination law, criminal law and health and safety law), whereas the CRPD's focus in Article 27 is on anti-discrimination law.[154] The FED's approach, in line with the EU's competence, relates to anti-discrimination law only, though member states have separate, independent obligations under the CRPD. Another consequence of the difference in approach is that the ILO Convention does not require a victim of violence or harassment to demonstrate less favourable treatment based on disability, with the difficulties that may entail; rather, it is sufficient simply that they have been harassed. This may help to overcome the difficulties with comparison identified in relation to anti-discrimination law,[155] though it also may mean that some harms associated

---

[153] ILO, in note 136, [19].

[154] Art 27 of the CRPD mentions health and safety, and the scope of Art 16 would encompass criminal law also. Criminal sanctions are also referenced in CESCR, in note 10, [48].

[155] See, for example, Suzanne B. Goldberg, 'Discrimination by comparison' (2011) 120 *The Yale Law Journal*, 728.

with discriminatory forms of harassment are overlooked, notwithstanding the ILO Convention's emphasis on harms caused.[156]

Both the CRPD (as interpreted in General Comment No. 6) and the FED adopt a purely subjective test to harassment, as it is sufficient if either the 'purpose or effect' of the harassment is to violate dignity or create 'an intimidating, hostile, degrading, humiliating or offensive environment' for that person.[157] By contrast, it appears that the test under the ILO Convention is both subjective and objective, meaning that a reasonable person, as well as the victim, must consider the behaviour unacceptable. In a social environment where disability harassment is normalized,[158] this test is potentially problematic.

Both the CRPD and the ILO Convention emphasize the importance of an intersectional approach, an issue that remains problematic under the FED. It follows that the CRPD and ILO Convention have far greater scope to address some key forms of disability harassment, both as regards the nature of harassment itself, and in terms of addressing structural and attitudinal barriers to effective complaint. However, unlike the other two instruments, the ILO Convention does not reference shifting the burden of proof, though this is mentioned in the accompanying Recommendation No. 206.[159]

The main advance of the ILO Convention is the sheer breadth of the working context it considers. Addressing the 'world of work', the ILO Convention defines this extremely broadly and in great detail, addressing multiple work-related contexts, such as commuting and digital media, as well as

---

[156] For example, the psychological impact of harassment based on group affinity may not be recognized under health and safety approaches.

[157] CRPD Committee, in note 52, [18(d)]; FED, Article 2(3).

[158] See the discussion in Section 3.2.

[159] ILO, in note 136, [16].

formal and informal labour.[160] In this sense, it is broader even than Article 27 of the CRPD, which addresses discrimination in 'all forms of employment' but does not look beyond this to the broader working environment. The FED addresses 'employment and occupation'[161] in the public and private sectors,[162] though member states may exclude the armed forces.[163] It does not address work-related spaces.

The ILO Convention and Recommendation No. 206 offer a detailed account of what states must do to address work-related harassment and violence, both in terms of legislation and in terms of awareness-raising and training. In this regard, they resemble the CRPD rather than the FED, which focuses more on the outcome to be achieved than the means of achieving it. However, the ILO Convention has an advantage over the CRPD, as it is a labour convention, drafted with specific reference to the labour context by participants highly experienced in that field. This enables it to identify issues and mechanisms that are generally overlooked by the CRPD.[164] For example, Article 8 of the ILO Convention requires states to identify 'in consultation with the employers' and workers' organizations concerned and through other means, the sectors or occupations and work arrangements in which workers and other persons concerned are more exposed to violence and harassment'. Similarly, Article 10 requires them to:

ensure that labour inspectorates and other relevant authorities, as appropriate, are empowered to deal with

---

[160] ILO Convention, Art 3.

[161] FED, Art 1.

[162] Ibid, Art 3.

[163] Ibid, Art 3.

[164] Some points included in the ILO Convention are echoed in the 'Draft general comment on Article 27' regarding the CRPD, though not in Art 27 of the CRPD itself. CRPD Committee, in note 63, [29], [32], [85].

violence and harassment in the world of work, including by issuing orders requiring measures with immediate executory force, and orders to stop work in cases of an imminent danger to life, health or safety, subject to any right of appeal to a judicial or administrative authority which may be provided by law.

The ILO Convention also highlights the importance of employee voice and consultation with worker organizations.[165]

Finally, the ILO Convention's emphasis not only on accountability for perpetrators, but also on remedial actions, such as perpetrator counselling, is highly unusual. This represents a significant departure from the CRPD and the FED, which focus on prevention and redress in a general sense but do not require accountability for perpetrators. This may be due to the broader scope of the ILO Convention, which addresses not only criminal forms of violence and harassment, but also the civil law context addressed in the FED and in Article 27 of the CRPD.[166] The ILO Convention's approach differs from much anti-discrimination legislation, which typically focuses on employer liability, rather than accountability for perpetrators, both because employers control the employment context and (possibly) because many perpetrators may lack the resources for meaningful recompense. The ILO Convention also focuses explicitly on third-party harassment,[167] unlike the CRPD and the FED. Arguably, the reference to 'protection from harassment' in Article 27 should encompass this; Article 2 of the FED is more opaque, but third-party harassment could potentially

---

[165] For example, ILO Convention, Arts 9, 11.

[166] It should be noted, however, that Art 16 of the CRPD, which addresses violence and exploitation more generally, focuses on prevention and protection, rather than accountability.

[167] ILO Convention, Art 4.

come within the blanket prohibition on discrimination in Article 2(1).[168]

2.7 Conclusion

This chapter has outlined some of the principal ways in which the human rights framework addresses disability, either explicitly or implicitly. It also highlights the potential of this framework to address disability harassment specifically, even prior to the more specialized provisions in the CRPD, FED and ILO Convention. The chapter has demonstrated the importance increasingly accorded by human rights instruments and their committees to intersectional analysis, particularly in relation to gender, though also encompassing other intersecting characteristics, such as race.

The chapter has also explored three of the most significant instruments for addressing disability harassment at work in the European and global contexts. Highlighting the broad scope of the CRPD, the chapter contrasted the approach of the CRPD with that of the FED, identifying significant similarities and differences. Of these, the most important differences in practice are likely to be the continuing fractures between the conceptualization of disability in both instruments (which may result in significantly narrower protection under the FED, even in the employment context) and the failure of the FED, to date, to address intersectional forms of discrimination, including harassment. These differences are particularly important, as many EU member states may incorrectly assume that transposing the FED into

---

[168] This states: 'For the purposes of this Directive, the "principle of equal treatment" shall mean that there shall be no direct or indirect discrimination whatsoever on any of the grounds referred to in Article 1.' Art 2(3) then construes harassment as a form of discrimination within the meaning of this paragraph.

national law is sufficient to meet their CRPD obligations. This possibility is also noted by Waddington and Broderick in their detailed review of the CRPD and the FED.[169] Finally, the chapter has explored the potential of the ILO Convention to advance protection from work–related disability harassment. Greatly expanding the conceptualization of the 'world of work', the ILO Convention moves from a harassment approach based on discrimination to one based on human rights more broadly, and it discusses in detail how this can be promoted, holistically, in the specific context of labour and labour relations.

---

[169] Waddington and Broderick, in note 89, 89.

THREE

Barriers to Effective National Implementation

3.1 Introduction

The human rights framework outlined in Chapter Two requires states to take steps to address disability harassment. However, even where states do this (usually as an aspect of their general equality and anti-discrimination law), it does not necessarily follow that these measures are effective in practice. This is not to say that such measures are unimportant – they certainly provide an avenue for redress for some, and they communicate that disability harassment is unacceptable, thus performing an important normative function. Nevertheless, as this chapter demonstrates, equality legislation may achieve less than anticipated, as it does not generally address either the root causes of harassment or the underlying social and structural barriers to enforcement.

This chapter focuses on what Allott terms the 'curative effectiveness' of disability harassment law, that is, the extent to which law succeeds in rectifying an injustice.[1] As Mousmouti puts it, 'legislative effectiveness expresses the extent to which a law can do the job it is intended to do'.[2] She highlights 'the tension between the need for legislation to regulate complex social relationships and behaviours and the need to ensure

---

[1] Anthony Allott, 'The effectiveness of laws' (1981) 15 *Valparaiso University Law Review*, 229, 234.

[2] Maria Mousmouti, 'Effectiveness as an aspect of quality of EU legislation: is it feasible?' (2014) 2 *The Theory and Practice of Legislation*, 309, 311.

effectiveness in a tangible and measurable way' as particularly pertinent to equality legislation.[3] Since specific data on the effectiveness of disability harassment law are often lacking, the chapter also draws on research on the effectiveness of equality law more generally. The key focus is on whether victims of discrimination, particularly disability harassment, have meaningful access to effective legal remedies. This, in turn, requires a consideration of the barriers to justice experienced both in equality cases generally and by persons with disabilities specifically. The chapter also considers effectiveness in terms of outcomes, not only focusing on whether equality actions generally, and harassment actions specifically, are likely to be successful, but also identifying reasons for the failure of legal cases insofar as these are identified in research.

The chapter begins with an overview of the barriers to making equality and disability harassment complaints, followed by a discussion of the success rates for equality claims, including harassment claims. The chapter argues that even where legislation is adopted to address disability harassment, a wide range of social and structural barriers may discourage legal complaints. Furthermore, even where disability harassment claims are brought, the available evidence suggests that the rate of success is not high. Relatively little work has been done to establish the reasons for this, though general research on equality claims may be indicative. The chapter therefore highlights the importance of continued monitoring and research, as well as the need for disaggregated disability equality data.

3.2 Barriers to disability harassment complaints and legal claims

People who experience harassment or other forms of discrimination at work may use different means to address

---

[3] Ibid, 314.

this. These do not always involve legal complaint, as many employees (if they complain at all) may opt for formal or informal organizational complaint processes. This section examines some of the barriers to reporting disability harassment at work and, specifically, to making legal complaints.

International research suggests that few of those experiencing discrimination of any kind take legal action and that widespread social and structural barriers undermine legal effectiveness. For example, in the UK, the 2008 Fair Treatment at Work Survey found that only 4 per cent of respondents with disabilities applied to an employment tribunal, while 58 per cent tried to resolve the problem informally.[4] More recently, the 2021 UK Disability Survey found that although 58 per cent of respondents with disabilities reported being mistreated because of their disability, only 29 per cent of those who had experienced disability-related bullying, harassment or violence had officially reported it.[5] Reviewing the literature on the related issue of sexual harassment, McDonald notes that research data consistently indicate under-reporting by victims, either through internal or external complaints mechanisms.[6] More generally, the European Commission's most recent report on the Race Directive and the FED notes that under-reporting of discrimination remains a significant problem and that many

---

[4]   Nick Coleman, Wendy Sykes and Carola Groom, *Barriers to Employment and Unfair Treatment at Work: A Quantitative Analysis of Disabled People's Experiences* (EHRC 2013), 46.

[5]   Disability Unit, *UK Disability Survey Research Report, June 2021* (UK Government 2021), www.gov.uk/government/publications/uk-disabil ity-survey-research-report-june-2021/uk-disability-survey-research-rep ort-june-2021 (accessed 20 September 2021). This report did not address bullying or harassment in the work context specifically and much of the focus was on harassment or mistreatment in public spaces.

[6]   Paula McDonald, 'Workplace sexual harassment 30 years on: a review of the literature' (2011) 14 *International Journal of Management Reviews*, 1, 9.

victims of discrimination 'would not easily report the incident', undermining the effectiveness of the directives.[7] This follows on earlier reports that highlighted the low number of court cases[8] and the generally low level of rights awareness,[9] which led Mousmouti to conclude that 'while there is no doubt that results have been achieved at the level of legal remedies, it is obscure whether or what results have been achieved in real life' by the directives.[10]

All this is unsurprising: there are multiple reasons why employees may fail to seek recourse for discrimination through legislative processes. Areheart identifies reluctance to believe that discrimination is the cause of a particular work outcome, fear of retaliation and fear of poor outcomes if a complaint is made – or, at least, a lack of confidence in a positive outcome or effective resolution – as among the factors affecting legal complaint.[11] To this may be added concerns about the financial and personal costs of making a legal complaint, concerns

---

[7] European Commission, 'Report on the application of Council Directive 2000/43/EC implementing the principle of equal treatment between persons irrespective of racial or ethnic origin ("the Racial Equality Directive") and of Council Directive 2000/78/EC establishing a general framework for equal treatment in employment and occupation ("the Employment Equality Directive")' (Com No. 139 final, 2021), [2.2.1].

[8] European Commission, 'The application of Directive 2000/78/EC of 27 November 2000 establishing a general framework for equal treatment in employment and occupation' (Com No. 225 final/2, 2008).

[9] European Commission, 'Joint report on the application of Council Directive 2000/43/EC of 29 June 2000 implementing the principle of equal treatment between persons irrespective of racial or ethnic origin ("Racial Equality Directive") and of Council Directive 2000/78/EC of 27 November 2000 establishing a general framework for equal treatment in employment and occupation ("Employment Equality Directive")' (COM [2014] 2 final).

[10] Mousmouti, in note 2, 324.

[11] Bradley A. Areheart, 'Organizational justice and antidiscrimination' (2020) 104 *Minnesota Law Review*, 1921.

about the adversarial nature and complexity of the process,[12] limited rights awareness, short timelines for filing complaints and (sometimes) the chilling effects of internal complaints processes and procedures.[13]

Many of these issues are also highlighted in other research. For example, in its recent guidance on sexual and work-related harassment in the UK, the EHRC highlights reporting barriers, such as a belief that an employer would not take the matter seriously or would protect the alleged perpetrator (particularly senior staff), as well as a fear of victimization and a lack of appropriate procedures.[14] Similarly, in its detailed report on sexual harassment in the UK, the Women and Equalities Committee highlights 'cost and inequality of arms' as 'the greatest barrier to pursuing a case',[15] and notes that low compensation awards also deter complaints.[16] The European Commission has likewise emphasized the importance of alleviating the financial burden of proceedings for applicants, including by reducing court fees in relation to discrimination claims, as well as through other measures, such as providing funds in advance for legal costs.[17] The European Commission has also highlighted the importance of rights awareness, noting that victims of discrimination may be unaware of their rights or of the existence of equality bodies (or, presumably, complaints

---

[12] Frances McGinnity, Raffaele Grotti, Helen Russell and Oona Kenny, *Who Experiences Discrimination in Ireland? Evidence from the QNHS Equality Modules* (Irish Human Rights and Equality Commission 2017), 10.

[13] Areheart, in note 11, 1935.

[14] EHRC, *Sexual Harassment and Harassment at Work: Technical Guidance* (EHRC 2020), https://equalityhumanrights.com/sites/default/files/sexual_harassment_and_harassment_at_work.pdf (accessed 19 October 2021).

[15] Women and Equalities Committee, *Sexual Harassment in the Workplace* (HC 2017–19, 725-I), 29.

[16] Ibid, 29–30.

[17] European Commission, in note 7, [2.2.1].

mechanisms).[18] The European Commission identified concrete issues that may impact on access to justice, particularly for marginalized groups, including short legal time limits for complaint, costly or complex proceedings, uncertainty as to outcomes, and the ultimate likelihood of low compensation.[19] Ineffective remedies may also be a concern, as the European Commission noted persistent difficulties with some national courts unduly limiting compensatory awards or favouring non-monetary compensation. This might discourage victims from taking appropriate legal action.[20]

Further systemic issues include the reliance on an individual enforcement model. Bornstein highlights that legal protections against discrimination and retaliation for complaint are often ineffective, as they rely on individual enforcement.[21] This assumes that individual victims of discrimination have the knowledge, means and resources, including the personal resilience and physical and emotional energy, to pursue what may be a lengthy, exhausting, high-risk and potentially low-reward complaint process. However, as noted previously, research strongly indicates that employees may have significant concerns about taking individual action. For this reason, Bornstein argues in favour of mandatory disclosure requirements for employers (such as public reporting obligations in relation to harassment cases) as a more effective means of enforcing anti-discrimination law by shifting at least some of the enforcement burden from individual employees to employers and government agencies.[22]

Attitudinal barriers may also arise and should not be underestimated. In a study of disability-related mistreatment at

---

[18] Ibid.

[19] Ibid.

[20] Ibid, [2.2.4].

[21] Stephanie Bornstein, 'Disclosing discrimination' (2021) 101 *Boston University Law Review*, 287.

[22] Ibid.

work, Koch et al highlight the common strategy of attempting to 'grin and bear it'.[23] This strategy was adopted for various reasons, such as a fear of not being believed, experiencing backlash or losing employment.[24] A further factor was that those who reported mistreatment felt that it did not resolve the problem and often made the situation worse.[25] Complaint can carry significant social costs; for instance, a study by Kaiser and Miller found that individuals who complained of discrimination were more negatively regarded by others, even where the discrimination complaint was clearly well founded.[26] They concluded that this might dissuade people from stigmatized groups from challenging discrimination, which might, in turn, be taken to indicate that discrimination was not a problem.[27]

Some general barriers impact particularly on employees with disabilities. For example, tribunal fees may disproportionately affect disability discrimination claims, as many persons with disabilities are in insecure or part-time employment.[28] This is evidenced by a recent significant rise in UK tribunal claims for disability discrimination following the abolition of fees.[29] The potential cost of legal action may particularly deter complaints

---

[23] Lynn C. Koch and others, 'On-the-job treatment of employees with disabilities: a grounded theory investigation' (2021) *Rehabilitation Counseling Bulletin*, 1, 8.

[24] Ibid, 9.

[25] Ibid.

[26] Cheryl R. Kaiser and Carol T. Miller, 'Stop complaining! The social costs of making attributions to discrimination' (2001) 27 *Personality and Social Psychology Bulletin*, 254, 261.

[27] Ibid, 262.

[28] J. Brown and A. Powell, 'Disabled people in employment', HC Library Briefing Paper 7540 (13 August 2020), 9; AHRC, *Respect@Work: Sexual Harassment National Inquiry Report* (AHRC 2020), 181.

[29] Jane Croft, 'Surge in disability discrimination cases at employment tribunals', *Financial Times* (2020), www.ft.com/content/a6b915a6-338d-11ea-a329-0bcf87a328f2 (accessed 18 November 2021).

where legal aid is unavailable.[30] Again, this may particularly affect those who are insecurely employed.

However, disability-specific and intersectional barriers also discourage complaints. Flynn has highlighted that persons with disabilities experience multiple barriers in accessing justice.[31] These barriers may be informational – for instance, persons with disabilities may be unable to obtain relevant information in an accessible format. They may also be attitudinal – resulting, for example, from assumptions regarding legal capacity. Less obvious barriers may include the lack of specialized knowledge on the part of legal professionals and difficulties accessing complaint mechanisms.[32] Accessibility in relation to court procedures can also pose significant challenges; this may include the physical accessibility of court or tribunal premises, as well as accessibility in relation to procedures and communication (for instance, the need for sign language interpretation or assistive technologies).[33]

Disability harassment is often normalized as inevitable and unavoidable.[34] This can lead to invisibility,[35] so that even victims of disability harassment may fail to identify it.[36] Fevre states that many employees with disabilities see ill-treatment 'as a normal aspect of their employment', rather than as disability-related discrimination.[37] Accordingly, harassment reporting 'is influenced not only by personal perception, but also by how

---

[30] Eilionóir Flynn, *Disabled Justice? Access to Justice and the UN Convention on the Rights of Persons with Disabilities* (Routledge 2016), 49.

[31] Ibid, chs 3, 4.

[32] Ibid, ch 3.

[33] Ibid, ch 4.

[34] EHRC, *Hidden in Plain Sight: Inquiry into Disability-Related Harassment* (EHRC 2011), 57.

[35] Ibid.

[36] Ibid, 57–8.

[37] Ralph Fevre, 'Why work is so problematic for people with disabilities and long-term health problems' (2017) 67 *Occupational Medicine*, 593.

it is defined in the cultural context and the level of individual awareness'.[38]

In a detailed report on disability harassment (albeit outside the employment context), the EHRC notes that victims of disability harassment (like victims of sexual harassment) may feel embarrassed, ashamed or guilty,[39] and may blame themselves for what happened.[40] These issues may be exacerbated by the emotional exhaustion of dealing with constant low-level harassment in daily life,[41] as well as concern about a potentially stressful complaints process.[42] For some respondents, form-filling itself may be a deterrent to complaint,[43] and there may also be accessibility issues.[44] Overall, the EHRC found that persons with disabilities were more likely to report harassment if it was indisputably serious[45] and they believed there was a realistic chance of achieving a desirable outcome.[46] A positive reporting experience (irrespective of outcome) could increase the likelihood of future reporting.[47] Although the EHRC's report focused on disability harassment outside of employment, there is no reason to suppose that these factors are less relevant within employment.

Many employees with conditions that would qualify as disabilities may not identify as 'disabled' or wish to disclose their impairment (for example, for fear of social

---

[38] Eurofound (2015) 'Violence and harassment in European workplaces: causes, impacts and policies', 10, www.eurofound.europa.eu/publications/report/2015/violence-and-harassment-in-european-workplaces-extent-impacts-and-policies (accessed 18 January 2022).

[39] EHRC, in note 34, 61–2.

[40] Ibid, 62.

[41] Ibid, 63, 65.

[42] Ibid, 95.

[43] Ibid, 98.

[44] Ibid, 100.

[45] Ibid.

[46] Ibid.

[47] Ibid, 101.

stigmatization).[48] They may therefore prefer not to make a disability complaint or may not perceive themselves as entitled to do so. The position is further complicated by intersectional considerations, as it may not be easy to identify a single ground of claim. For instance, a woman with a disability might identify harassment as being based on her gender, age or race, rather than her disability. Fevre et al surmise that the comparatively low reporting rate for disability and religious discrimination in the UK indicates a greater reluctance to classify less favourable treatment as discrimination in these contexts.[49] However, there may also be tactical reasons for pursuing a case under a particular heading only. Apart from the failure of much equality legislation to address intersectionality, research suggests that claims involving multiple or intersectional forms of discrimination are less likely to be successful in practice. This is discussed further in Section 3.3.

Women with disabilities face particular concerns in relation to reporting sexual harassment. Some of these additional barriers relate specifically to employment, while others are more general. As Buckley notes, persons with disabilities are generally much less likely to be employed than persons without disabilities, and women with disabilities are less likely to be employed than men with disabilities. This directly contributes to higher poverty rates for persons with disabilities and, specifically, for women with disabilities. In this global context, fear of loss of employment can be a very significant barrier to complaint.[50] Similar concerns are expressed in a

---

[48] Michael J. Prince, 'Persons with invisible disabilities and workplace accommodation: findings from a scoping literature review' (2017) 46 *Journal of Vocational Rehabilitation*, 75, 80.

[49] Ralph Fevre and others, *Fair Treatment at Work Report: Findings from the 2008 Survey* (Department for Business, Innovation and Skills 2009), 210–11.

[50] Lucy-Ann Buckley, 'Women with disabilities forever on the edge of #MeToo?', in Ann M. Noel and David B. Oppenheimer (eds),

recent report by UN Women on the sexual harassment of women with disabilities. Women in that research indicated that they do not report harassment to avoid being perceived as 'troublemakers', or as 'overly demanding', in case this impacted on their employment security. The report highlights that this fear is particularly high for women with disabilities given that employment rates for this cohort are particularly low.[51]

Richardson and Taylor highlight that the cost–benefit analysis involved in deciding whether to complain may differ for particular social groups, referring to 'conditioned credibility concerns' that are 'socially constructed within society and spill over into organisational contexts'.[52] While their research focuses on issues of gender and race, equivalent challenges apply in relation to disability. Employees with psychosocial disabilities may have a well-grounded apprehension that they will not be believed if they complain about harassment.[53] Buckley notes that this particularly applies to women with psychosocial conditions, who are typically seen as unreliable witnesses.[54] Women with disabilities may also be perceived as either asexual or hyper-sexual, with either belief serving to undermine complaints of sexual harassment.[55] The recent report by UN Women on sexual harassment of women with disabilities notes that 'the general culture of disbelief in women is sharper for women with disabilities, as credibility diminishes

    Globalization of the #MeToo Movement (Fastcase and Full Court Press 2020), 424.

[51] Rosario Grima Algora and Purna Sen, *Sexual Harassment against Women with Disabilities in the Work Place and on Campus* (UN Women 2020), 14.

[52] Brian Richardson and Juandalynn Taylor, 'Sexual harassment at the intersection of race and gender: a theoretical model of the sexual harassment experiences of women of color' (2009) 73 *Western Journal of Communication*, 248.

[53] EHRC, in note 34, 109.

[54] Buckley, in note 50, 428.

[55] Ibid, 427–8.

when social structures of inequality intersect'.[56] The report highlights different ways that women with disabilities can be excluded from justice, either because they are infantilized or because they are discredited (especially those with psychosocial or intellectual disabilities) or considered unreliable witnesses (for example, due to hearing or visual impairments, so that they cannot give evidence as to what they saw or heard). The report notes that 'Judges may require more corroborating evidence for women with disabilities than for women without disabilities, especially where psychosocial or intellectual disabilities are present or when women require assistive communication or accommodations.'[57] It also notes that stereotypes and prejudicial assumptions regarding men with disabilities may likewise impact on access to justice, either by undermining their complaints of sexual assault or harassment, or because it is assumed that they could not have perpetrated a sexual assault.[58]

Buckley also highlights that accepted concepts of sexual harassment and legal framings can be problematic for groups whose experiences are different.[59] For example, women with disabilities experience not only rape and sexual abuse, but also disability-specific forms of coercive control that may have a sexual or gender-based dimension. These may include, for example, interference with mobility or mobility aids, or with communication aids or technologies.[60] While such forms of

---

[56] Grima Algora and Sen, in note 51, 14.

[57] Ibid, 19.

[58] Ibid.

[59] Buckley, in note 50, 428. Similar research in Canada highlights differences in the racial experience of sexual harassment and the relative ability to complain and seek legal redress. Sandy Welsh, Jacquie Carr, Barbara MacQuarrie and Audrey Huntley, '"I'm not thinking of it as sexual harassment": understanding harassment across race and citizenship', (2006) 20 *Gender & Society*, 87.

[60] Buckley, in note 50, 430.

harassment may be dealt with simply as disability harassment, this may fail to understand or address the full harm suffered.

3.3 Success rates for equality claims

Even where legal cases are brought, the available evidence suggests that the success rate for equality claims is quite low.[61] This appears to apply across jurisdictions and across different forms of discrimination, including equality claims generally, disability discrimination claims generally and harassment and sexual harassment cases. This section outlines the available data and explores the reasons identified in the literature for the low success of disability equality and harassment claims.

A range of literature on discrimination claims in the US highlights varying success rates in different forums, though nearly all of these were less than 40 per cent, and many were far lower.[62] Outcomes in alternative dispute resolution forums were not necessarily more successful; reviewing discrimination claims generally, Gough highlights that outcomes in mandatory arbitration cases were 'starkly inferior' to those in traditional civil litigation, concluding that 'Employees are less likely to win, they receive smaller awards, and they receive a smaller proportion of claim amounts in arbitration relative to state and federal trials.'[63] In relation to disability discrimination, an early study by Colker, analysing the outcomes of 720 cases in the first eight years after the passing of the Americans with Disabilities Act (ADA), highlighted an extremely low rate of success. Colker found

---

[61] Many legal complaints may not proceed to hearing, with many cases being abandoned, withdrawn, dismissed or settled (discussed further in Chapters Five and Six).

[62] For a summary overview, see Mark Gough, 'A tale of two forums: employment discrimination outcomes in arbitration and litigation' (2021) 74(4) *ILR Review*, 875.

[63] Ibid, 892.

that 87 per cent of cases resulted in dismissals or summary judgments in favour of employers, and that the success rate for employers in district courts was 94 per cent. She noted that employers were successful in 83–9 per cent of cases during the period of study.[64] On the other hand, a 2005 study of the impact of the ADA by Moss et al found that settlements were significantly beneficial to ADA claimants but that the 'vast majority' of persons eligible to bring a claim did not do so.[65] They concluded that the greatest barrier to plaintiffs was 'the increasingly narrow judicial interpretation of the ADA'.[66] An analysis by Konur of the UK's Disability Discrimination Act 1995 indicated a greater rate of successful claims than under the ADA, though the success rate was still not high. Konur found that employers were successful in 63 per cent of cases, largely for jurisdictional and procedural reasons, as well as issues related to disability tests.[67]

In a recent Australian analysis, Blackham highlights that age discrimination claims in Australia are 'notoriously unsuccessful'.[68] She concludes that while many cases are resolved through conciliation,[69] the lack of success at hearing was partly due to 'procedural and substantive hurdles' that limit success even where cases are not particularly weak.[70] Key issues included short time limits, difficulties proving causation, lack

---

[64] Ruth Colker, 'Winning and losing under the Americans with Disabilities Act' (2001) 62 *Ohio State Law Journal*, 239.

[65] Kathryn Moss, Michael Ullman, Jeffrey W. Swanson, Leah M. Ranney and Scott Burris, 'Prevalence and outcomes of ADA employment discrimination claims in the federal courts' (2005) 29 *Mental & Physical Disability Law Reporter*, 303.

[66] Ibid, 307.

[67] Ozcan Konur, 'A judicial outcome analysis of the Disability Discrimination Act: a windfall for employers?' (2007) 22 *Disability & Society*, 187.

[68] Alysia Blackham, 'Why do employment age discrimination cases fail? An analysis of Australian case law' (2020) 42 *Sydney Law Review*, 1, 2.

[69] Ibid, 3.

[70] Ibid, 2.

of evidence and claims beyond the scope of the legislation.[71] Similarly, in a recent analysis of age discrimination claims in the UK, Blackham found that the 'vast majority' of such claims were also unsuccessful in employment tribunals.[72] In practice, most claims were withdrawn prior to hearing (either settled or abandoned), but those progressing to hearing were unlikely to succeed. This caused Blackham to question the individual enforcement model, though she notes the difficulties in assessing its effectiveness in practice given the very limited data collected or published by tribunals.[73] This especially applies to data applicable to particular demographic groups, including those experiencing intersectional discrimination. Blackham particularly identifies issues with time limits, which may be too short for many individuals to identify what they are experiencing, seek advice and initiate discrimination claims, especially where they engage first in internal complaint processes.[74] She further highlights that 'for many claimants, managing a discrimination claim is *on top of* the already onerous process of finding a new job, or navigating a discriminatory or toxic workplace on a day-to-day basis'.[75] While it may be possible to obtain an extension of time, this often requires claimants to reveal highly personal information, which then becomes a matter of public record. Blackham questions the statutory preference for short time limits, noting that, in practice, 'Extensive delays undermine key arguments in favour of time limits', such as ensuring a timely resolution or protecting the quality and availability of evidence.[76]

---

[71] Ibid.

[72] Alysia Blackham, 'Enforcing rights in employment tribunals: insights from age discrimination claims in a new "dataset"' (2021) 41(3) *Legal Studies*, 390.

[73] Ibid, 392.

[74] Ibid, 404.

[75] Ibid.

[76] Ibid.

In relation to harassment claims specifically, an early UK study of 155 sexual harassment cases heard between 1995 and 2005 found that slightly more than half of claims that made it to a final hearing were likely to be upheld.[77] A later study by Lockwood and Marda found that almost half of UK work-related harassment cases in their sample were successful at hearing,[78] but their analysis does not give disaggregated figures for disability.[79] By contrast, the EHRC found that disability discrimination claims had a low success rate at hearing in the UK,[80] suggesting that disability harassment claims are also unlikely to succeed. The UK findings, though mixed, nevertheless compare quite favourably with the US, where Weber's pioneering study found that the 'vast majority' of disability harassment cases taken under the ADA were unsuccessful. This was primarily due to restrictive judicial interpretation.[81]

Lockwood and Marda's analysis of UK cases found that complaints relating to physical harassment were more likely to succeed than claims relating to verbal harassment only.[82] They also found that claimants who availed of formal grievance processes were more likely to succeed than those who did not,[83]

---

[77] Patrice Rosenthal and Alexandra Budjanovcanin, 'Sexual harassment judgments by British employment tribunals 1995–2005: implications for claimants and their advocates' (2011) 49 *British Journal of Industrial Relations*, s236, s248.

[78] Graeme Lockwood and Vidushi Marda, 'Harassment in the workplace: the legal context' (2014) 31 *Jurisprudence*, 667, 672.

[79] In another UK study of disability discrimination cases, 28 per cent of disability harassment claims were successful, but the sample size was tiny (seven cases). Graeme Lockwood, Claire Henderson and Graham Thornicroft, 'Challenging mental health discrimination in employment' (2013) 17 *Journal of Workplace Rights*, 137, 141.

[80] Coleman et al, in note 4, 60–1.

[81] Mark C. Weber, *Disability Harassment* (New York University Press 2007), 26.

[82] Lockwood and Marda, in note 78, 672.

[83] Ibid.

as were those who could offer more detailed evidence.[84] Other relevant factors included the presence of an equal opportunities policy that included a formal grievance resolution policy.[85] Strikingly, claimants who brought additional or multiple claims were least likely to be successful.[86] This echoes similar findings by Rosette et al in the US that compound or intersectional discrimination claims are less successful than those based on single characteristics and that women of colour are only half as likely to succeed in discrimination cases generally, as compared to White women.[87] This comparative lack of success may be, as Lockwood and Marda suggest, because a multiplicity of claims undermines a claimant's credibility in the eyes of the adjudicator.[88] However, it may also be because the synergistic nature of intersectional forms of harassment can prove problematic in legal analysis. In this regard, Fredman notes that claims based on multiple forms of discrimination (for instance, claims of both racial and disability harassment) can be accommodated within existing legal frameworks, which are usually based on a single axis, as each type of discrimination can be analysed separately in relation to a single characteristic. Synergistic forms of discrimination are more difficult to address, as the disadvantage does not seem to relate to individual protected characteristics.[89]

---

[84] Ibid, 673.

[85] Ibid.

[86] Ibid.

[87] Ashleigh Shelby Rosette et al, 'Intersectionality: connecting experiences of gender with race at work' (2018) 38 *Research in Organizational Behavior*, 1.

[88] Lockwood and Marda, in note 78, 678.

[89] Directorate-General for Justice and Consumers (European Commission), European Network of Legal Experts in Gender Equality and Non-discrimination and Sandra Fredman, *Intersectional Discrimination in EU Gender Equality and Non-discrimination Law* (Publications Office of the European Union 2016), 7.

3.4 Conclusion

This chapter has highlighted that national legislative measures to address disability harassment at work may be relatively ineffective in practice. The first issue is that many persons with disabilities may be reluctant to avail of internal complaints procedures or legal redress mechanisms. This is often due to attitudinal barriers, which may be internal or external. Internal barriers may include: lack of rights awareness; feelings of shame or self-blame; fear of disbelief or of making things worse; a belief that complaints are unlikely to succeed or to attract worthwhile remedies; and failure to identify conduct as disability harassment due to the normalization of this kind of behaviour. External barriers include prevailing social attitudes (such as a failure to construe disability harassment as problematic or stereotypes about persons with disabilities) and structural considerations that have a practical impact on the ability to complain. The latter include: the lack of accessible information and complaint mechanisms; the cost and duration of legal complaint processes; short timelines for complaint; inadequate remedies; and rules on legal capacity. Particular barriers apply to women with disabilities and other intersectional groups. These may again be not only attitudinal (such as a belief that women with psychosocial disabilities are unreliable witnesses or are hyper-sexual), but also structural (such as legal framings of sexual harassment that do not take account of the experiences of women with disabilities). As discussed in Chapter Six, these problems may require (at least) systemic intervention to address particular barriers to complaint, as well as, potentially, the development of alternative or supplementary means to address disability harassment.

The second issue is that even where disability harassment complaints are brought, the available evidence suggests that they are unlikely to succeed at hearing. This evidence is very incomplete, however, and is drawn from a limited number of jurisdictions. We have some data on the outcome of equality complaints generally or in relation to specific kinds of discrimination claims (such as age discrimination). We also have limited evidence on the outcome of disability discrimination claims generally and on harassment or sexual harassment cases generally. However, we have minimal information on the outcome of disability harassment cases specifically.[90] From an intersectional perspective, the available data suggest that cases involving multiple grounds of claim are particularly unlikely to succeed. Again, however, these data are limited. This clearly indicates a need for specific, disaggregated data on the outcome of disability harassment complaints and regular monitoring of case outcomes to establish if there are reasons for concern.

---

[90] The main exception is Weber's analysis of US disability harassment cases, in note 81.

FOUR

Disability Harassment in Ireland

4.1 Introduction

This chapter outlines the social and legal context for disability harassment in Ireland. Ireland is a member of the EU; as such, it is bound by EU law, including the FED, making it a suitable comparator for other EU member states or for states with an EU legal legacy, such as the UK. It has also ratified the CRPD, making its experience relevant to the many jurisdictions that have ratified that convention. Ireland's legislative provisions on disability harassment are comprehensive and, in most respects, exemplify compliance with both the FED and the CRPD. The Irish experience thus offers an excellent case study for the impact of disability harassment legislation in practice.

The chapter begins by outlining the available data on disability harassment in Ireland, the rate of legal complaints and the barriers to the exercise of legal complaint mechanisms. This section argues that while research on the Irish experience is limited, the available data suggest general alignment with the international findings outlined in Chapters One and Three, with some caveats. The chapter then outlines the Irish legislation addressing disability harassment at work – the Employment Equality Acts 1998–2021 (EEA) – and evaluates this for compliance with the FED and CRPD. It argues that while Irish law complies with (and indeed exceeds) FED standards, it falls short of CRPD requirements. The chapter concludes by outlining some of the key structural factors influencing the practical operation of the EEA, including the tribunal system.

4.2 Prevalence of disability harassment in Ireland

Recent figures show that 13.5 per cent of the Irish population has a disability,[1] and persons with disabilities are significantly disadvantaged in the labour market. Persons with disabilities have lower employment rates[2] and are disadvantaged in terms of occupational attainment.[3] However, there is almost no information on disability harassment. Some general data on employment discrimination are available, including a recent report by McGinnity et al analysing equality data gathered by the Central Statistics Office (CSO) in 2019. This highlights that 14 per cent of respondents with disabilities reported perceived discrimination in the workplace, compared with 7 per cent of respondents without disabilities.[4] Women, members of minority ethnic groups, non-Irish nationals and non-Catholics also reported higher rates of employment-related discrimination than average.[5]

The CSO notes that bullying or harassment was the most common work-related issue reported in its 2019 survey, cited

---

[1] Central Statistics Office (CSO), *Census of Population 2016 – Profile 9 Health, Disability and Carers* (Central Statistics Office 2017), www.cso.ie/en/releasesandpublications/ep/p-cp9hdc/p8hdc/ (accessed 29 May 2020).

[2] Recent data indicate that less than half (41 per cent) of persons with disabilities of working age in Ireland were employed, compared with over three quarters (78 per cent) of those without disabilities. Frances McGinnity, Helen Russell, Ivan Privalko and Shannen Enright, *Monitoring Decent Work in Ireland* (ESRI Research Series 2021), 47.

[3] Ibid, 57.

[4] Ibid, 105. The CSO survey definition of 'in the workplace' includes while looking for work. Figures relate to perceived experiences of discrimination in the previous two years. It should be noted that the CSO headline data appear to give slightly different figures: see CSO, *CSO Statistical Release – Equality and Discrimination 2019* (Central Statistics Office 2020), www.cso.ie/en/releasesandpublications/er/ed/equalityandiscrimination2019/ (accessed 28 May 2020).

[5] McGinnity et al, in note 2, 124.

by almost a third of respondents,[6] though the proportion of persons with disabilities reporting this is not specified. To date, national workplace bullying surveys have not addressed disability.[7] An analysis of ill-treatment and bullying in the workplace by Hogan et al did not find that disability was significantly associated with ill-treatment at work.[8] However, there is also strong evidence of prejudicial attitudes in Ireland towards persons with disabilities,[9] and disability is linked to significantly higher rates of domestic abuse[10] and repeated incidents of sexual violence outside the workplace.[11] A report

---

[6] CSO, in note 4. However, Hogan et al note that previous studies of workplace bullying in Ireland suggest that it may be less prevalent than in other jurisdictions. Victoria Hogan, Margaret Hodgins, Duncan Lewis, Sarah MacCurtain, Patricia Mannix-McNamara and Lisa Pursell, 'The prevalence of ill-treatment and bullying at work in Ireland' (2020) 13 *International Journal of Workplace Health Management*, 245, 246–7.

[7] See, for example, Philip J. O'Connell, Emma Calvert and Dorothy Watson, *Bullying in the Workplace: Survey Reports 2007* (Department of Enterprise, Trade and Employment 2007), 9, www.esri.ie/publi cations/bullying-in-the-workplace-survey-reports-2007 (accessed 23 November 2021).

[8] Hogan et al, in note 6, 258. The study did not address harassment specifically, but drew on the British Workplace Behaviour Study to focus on three broad factors: unreasonable management; incivility and disrespect; and violence and injury (Hogan et al, in note 6, 249).

[9] Helen Russell, Frances McGinnity, Emma Quinn and Rebecca King O'Riain, 'The experience of discrimination in Ireland: evidence from self-report data', in Laurence Bond, Frances McGinnity and Helen Russell (eds), *Making Equality Count: Irish and International Research Measuring Equality and Discrimination* (The Liffey Press 2010), 41.

[10] National Women's Council of Ireland, *A Review of Data on the Prevalence of Sexual Violence and Harassment of Women Students in Higher Education* (National Women's Council of Ireland 2017), 29, www.nwci.ie/ images/uploads/ESHTE_Report-Ireland_FINAL.pdf (accessed 19 January 2022).

[11] Helen Bartlett and Elaine Mears, *Sexual Violence against People with Disabilities: Data Collection and Barriers to Disclosure* (Rape Crisis Network Ireland 2012), 9.

on sexual violence against persons with disabilities indicates a higher rate of sexual violence for women with disabilities, particularly those with sensory or psychosocial disabilities,[12] than for women without disabilities.[13] Overall, therefore, the available evidence suggests that harassment is likely to be an issue for persons with disabilities at work in Ireland and that intersectional forms of harassment are also likely to arise.

The rate of legal discrimination complaints in Ireland aligns with the international picture of relatively few formal complaints. McGinnity et al estimate the rate of bringing a legal complaint at 10 per cent,[14] while Russell et al suggest it may be less than 6 per cent.[15] The social groups experiencing the most discrimination are the least likely to take action, possibly due to language issues, lack of confidence and lack of rights awareness.[16] A recent CSO survey found that over 70 per cent of people who experienced discrimination in the previous two years took no action,[17] while only 3 per cent made an official complaint.[18]

Although research on the barriers to legal complaint in Ireland is not extensive, many of the issues identified in the international research are likely to apply. For instance, financial costs have been identified as one of the most significant barriers to litigation in Ireland.[19] Other barriers include the adversarial

---

[12] Ibid.

[13] Ibid, 10.

[14] Frances McGinnity, Raffaele Grotti, Helen Russell and Oona Kenny, *Who Experiences Discrimination in Ireland? Evidence from the QNHS Equality Modules* (Irish Human Rights and Equality Commission 2017), 10.

[15] Russell et al, in note 9, 39.

[16] Ibid.

[17] CSO, in note 4.

[18] Ibid.

[19] Mel Cousins, 'How public interest law and litigation can make a difference to marginalised and vulnerable groups in Ireland', paper presented at the 'Public Interest Law in Ireland – The Reality and the Potential FLAC' conference, Dublin, 2005.

nature and complexity of the process,[20] as well as limited rights awareness and short timelines for filing complaints (discussed in Section 3.2). All of these difficulties may be compounded by inability to access representation, particularly given the unavailability of legal aid in most employment law cases.

Like the international research, Irish research indicates that reporting harassment and abuse is particularly problematic for persons with disabilities. O'Sullivan and MacMahon note that the need to make written submissions could deter potential claimants, particularly those from marginalized groups, including those with particular disabilities.[21] Research on sexual violence by Rape Crisis Network Ireland (RCNI) highlights additional difficulties where the abuser is a carer or in a position of authority, or where a complaints mechanism is inaccessible.[22] The main barriers to reporting identified by the RCNI were fear of being blamed for the violence, fear of not being believed and fear of the abuser.[23] Analysing qualitative data on the experiences of persons with disabilities who had experienced sexual violence, the RCNI found that 71 per cent had never been asked if they had suffered sexual violence, while 48 per cent (and 71 per cent of men) had never received information on potential avenues of support.[24] Respondents experienced disbelief and sometimes additional violence when they reported their experiences. Sometimes, they were able to make a partial disclosure only.[25] While the

---

[20] McGinnity et al, in note 14, 10.
[21] Michelle O'Sullivan and Juliet MacMahon, 'Employment equality legislation in Ireland: claimants, representation and outcomes' (2010) 39 *Industrial Law Journal*, 329, 338.
[22] Rape Crisis Network Ireland (RCNI) (2011), 'Sexual violence against people with disabilities: data collection and barriers to disclosure', 10, http://hdl.handle.net/10147/231913 (accessed 23 November 2021).
[23] Ibid.
[24] Ibid.
[25] Ibid.

RCNI's findings do not relate specifically to employment, many of the barriers identified may apply across contexts, including the work environment.

Finally, while this book focuses on harassment rather than hate crime, it should be noted that Irish legislation does not address hate crime, and current Irish hate speech legislation does not encompass disability.[26] Disability as a motivating factor for crime has been recordable since 2015,[27] and non-criminal hate incidents have been recordable since 2020.[28] However, as Haynes and Schweppe note, under-reporting and under-recording remain problematic,[29] and the very limited data available from official police statistics are not regarded as robust.[30]

4.3 Disability harassment in Irish employment equality law

Disability harassment at work is actionable in Ireland under the EEA. There are two potential heads of claim. First, a complaint may be brought under s 14A – a specific provision addressing harassment and sexual harassment. Second, a discrimination complaint may be made under s 6 (a general prohibition on discrimination) and/or s 8 (addressing discrimination relating to the terms and conditions of employment, or in relation to

---

[26] Prohibition of Incitement to Hatred Act 1989, discussed in Amanda Haynes and Jennifer Schweppe, *Lifecycle of a Hate Crime: Country Report for Ireland* (ICCL 2017), 15

[27] Ibid, 18.

[28] Office for Democratic Institutions and Human Rights (ODIHR), 'Hate crime reporting', https://hatecrime.osce.org/ireland (accessed 21 November 2021).

[29] Haynes and Schweppe, in note 26, 19.

[30] CSO, 'Crime and justice' (April 2019), www.cso.ie/en/statistics/crim eandjustice/ (accessed 20 November 2021); CSO, 'Recorded crime detection 2019: statistics under reservation', www.cso.ie/en/releases andpublications/ep/p-rcd/recordedcrimedetection2019/statisticsunder reservation/ (accessed 20 November 2021).

access to employment or promotion). The elements of these claims differ, but each requires the complainant (as the claimant is referred to)[31] to demonstrate a disability within the meaning of the EEA.

Establishing a disability is relatively straightforward. 'Disability' is broadly defined and, in substance, encompasses physical, sensory, psychosocial and neurodivergent conditions, as well as learning disabilities, though these terms are not used.[32] The disability may be past, present, future or imputed (perceived), but there is no requirement to demonstrate that it has a particular duration or affects a person's ability to function. This removes significant difficulties facing claimants in some other jurisdictions, such as the UK, and greatly reduces complexity in practice.[33] Nevertheless, some limitations apply. The condition or impairment must be medically recognized; a medical certificate is normally sufficient to show this, but an unsupported assertion is not.[34] Some disabilities may also be self-evident. Failing a medical diagnosis (or a sufficiently obvious impairment), it is unlikely that a condition will be held to constitute a disability.[35] Furthermore, although the definition of disability is extremely broad, not all conditions fall within its scope; for instance, stress does not normally constitute a disability, though it may give rise to one where it has further effects (such as hypertension).[36] Minor illnesses or injuries are also excluded.[37]

---

[31] EEA, s 77(4)(a).

[32] EEA, s 2(1).

[33] The UK guidance on the meaning of disability runs to 59 pages. Office for Disability Issues, *Equality Act 2010 Guidance* (Office for Disabilities, HM Government 2010).

[34] *Mr A v A Hospital* DEC-E2012–192.

[35] Claire Bruton, Cliona Kimber and Marguerite Bolger, *Employment Equality Law* (2nd edn) (Round Hall 2012), 332.

[36] *A Government Department v A Worker* EDA094.

[37] *Mr A v A Hospital* DEC-E2012-192.

Section 14A covers harassment and sexual harassment in the workplace or course of employment, which is committed by the complainant's employer or co-workers, or by clients or business contacts of the employer. However, an employer is only liable for harassment by clients or business contacts where the perpetrator is someone 'with whom the employer might reasonably expect the victim to come into contact in the workplace or otherwise in the course of his or her employment'[38] *and* 'the circumstances of the harassment are such that the employer ought reasonably to have taken steps to prevent it'.[39] This would certainly include situations where previous incidents had been reported to the employer[40] but might also include occurrences witnessed by management.

Harassment under s 14A includes 'any form of unwanted conduct related to any of the discriminatory grounds'.[41] This may encompass *Coleman*-type situations, where the victim is harassed because of their association with a person with a disability.[42] Unwanted conduct that is not related to a discriminatory ground is not covered by the EEA,[43] though it may be actionable as bullying.[44] Sexual harassment is defined as 'any form of unwanted verbal, non-verbal or physical conduct of a sexual nature'.[45] A single incident may be sufficient to constitute harassment,[46] and differential treatment related

---

[38] EEA, s 14(a)(4).

[39] EEA, s 14A(1)(a)(iii).

[40] *McCarthy v ISS Ireland Limited (Trading as ISS Facility Services) & Anor* [2018] IECA 287.

[41] EEA, s 14A(7)(a)(i).

[42] Case C-306/06, *Coleman v Attridge Law* [2008] ECR I-5603; see also Section 2.4.

[43] Irish Human Rights and Equality Commission, 'Code of practice on harassment and sexual harassment at work' (2022), [37].

[44] Department of Enterprise, Trade and Employment, 'Code of practice for employers and employees on the prevention and resolution of bullying at work' (2021).

[45] EEA, s 14A(7)(a)(ii).

[46] See, for example, *Ms A v A Contract Cleaning Company* DEC–E2004–068.

to the victim's response to harassment is also covered. The test for harassment in the EEA is subjective, being based on whether 'the purpose or effect' of the conduct is to create an 'intimidating, hostile, degrading, humiliating or offensive environment' for the victim.[47]

Finally, a statutory defence applies where an employer takes 'such steps as are reasonably practicable' to prevent harassment occurring or to address it appropriately (the reasonable steps defence).[48] This normally requires the adoption and implementation of a harassment policy, including an appropriate investigation process, and taking steps to reverse any adverse effects of the harassment.[49]

There are advantages and disadvantages to both heads of claim. Section 14A (the specific provision on harassment) sets out the key elements and the scope of both harassment and sexual harassment. Unlike the discrimination provisions in s 6 and s 8, it does not require a comparator. However, case law has interpreted the phrase 'related to any of the discriminatory grounds' as requiring a clear 'nexus' between the discriminatory ground and the form of the unwanted behaviour.[50] For instance, abusive language that refers expressly to disability would suffice, whereas generic abusive language might not.[51] This interpretation is arguably incorrect, as harassment based on disability is clearly 'related' to it, even if the form of the harassment is not disability specific. Notably, the 'nexus' requirement is not identified in the (non-legally binding) code of practice. By contrast, a harassment claim brought under s 6 or s 8 (the discrimination provisions) does

---

[47] EEA, s 14A(7)(a).

[48] EEA, s 14A(2).

[49] See, for example, *Victor Kings Oluebube v CPL Solutions Limited t/a Flexsource Recruitment* [2020] ADJ-00024254.

[50] See, for example, *A Customer Care Representative v A Provider of Outsourced Customer Support to a Mobile Phone Operator* DEC-E2016-092, [4.10].

[51] See, for example, *A Female Employee v A Printing Company* DEC-E2008-022.

not require a clear nexus between the nature of the conduct and the discriminatory ground, but requires a comparator (actual or hypothetical).[52] The essence of this claim is to show that the complainant was treated less favourably than someone else because of their actual or imputed disability, or because of their association with a person with a disability.[53]

The time limit for claims under the EEA is short. Claims must be initiated within six months of the discrimination or harassment, or its most recent occurrence,[54] where separate acts or omissions 'are sufficiently connected so as to constitute a continuum'.[55] This may apply 'where the alleged acts can be considered as separate manifestations of the same disposition to discriminate and the most recent occurrence was within the time period specified in the Act'.[56] The time period may be extended to 12 months 'for reasonable cause',[57] but the complainant must apply for and justify this.[58]

Finally, remedies under the EEA are quite extensive. Where the complainant is employed, compensation may be awarded up to 104 weeks' remuneration, or €40,000 (whichever is greater); in other cases, compensation is limited to €13,000.[59] Respondents may also be ordered to take a specified 'course of action'.[60] This need not relate to the particular proceedings

---

[52] Section 6(1)(a) requires the claimant to show that they were treated less favourably than someone else 'is, has been or would be treated … on any of the grounds specified'.

[53] EEA, s 6(1)(b).

[54] EEA, s 77(5)(a).

[55] *Hurley v County Cork VEC* EDA1124.

[56] *County Louth VEC v Don Johnson* EDA0712.

[57] EEA, s 77(5)(b).

[58] *Cementation Skanska (Formerly Kvaerner Cementation) v Carroll* DWT0425.

[59] EEA, s 82. UK readers should note that there is no Irish equivalent of the Vento scale in relation to injury to feelings and psychiatric injury (*Vento v Chief Constable of West Yorkshire Police (No. 2)* [2002] EWCA Civ 1871).

[60] EEA, s 82.

and, in practice, often includes an order to implement or review an equality or harassment policy, or to provide equality training.[61]

4.4 Compliance with the FED and the CRPD

Although disability discrimination, including harassment, was prohibited under the EEA from 1998, the legislation was significantly revised following the adoption of the FED and the Race Directive.[62] Section 14A was introduced specifically in response to those directives, replacing two separate sections addressing sexual and other forms of harassment.[63] Section 14A adopts much of the language of the directives, including the definition of harassment. The subjective test for harassment is also taken from the directives and replaces the original statutory test, which contained both subjective and objective elements, that is, both the victim and a reasonable person must have found the harassment offensive or intimidating.[64] The EEA implements EU law in relation to the burden of proof, which shifts to the respondent where a complainant demonstrates a prima facie case.[65] The extensive range of remedies also appears to comply with the requirements of the FED (and indeed the CRPD) that remedies should be 'effective, proportionate and dissuasive'. Overall, the EEA clearly satisfies the requirements of the FED in terms of addressing disability harassment.

Compliance with the CRPD is less complete. Although Ireland ratified the CRPD in 2018, it has not yet revised the EEA in light of that ratification. However, the Irish Supreme Court has stated that, in line with the case law of the CJEU,

---

[61] See, for example, *A Manager of an English Language School v An Institute of Technology* DEC–E2007–019.

[62] Equality Act 2004.

[63] EEA 1998, s 23 and s 32, as enacted.

[64] EEA, s 23(3) and s 32(5), as enacted.

[65] EEA, s 85A.

the EEA must be interpreted as far as possible in compliance with the CRPD.[66] In fact, most of the CRPD's requirements are satisfied in relation to harassment, insofar as the EEA complies with EU law standards, which are generally CRPD compliant.[67] Indeed, in one respect, the EEA's compliance with the CRPD is arguably superior to that of EU law, as its definition of disability goes beyond that of the FED, as interpreted to date by the CJEU.[68] Although the EEA's definition of disability is primarily medical, based on categories of impairments, the CRPD Committee has clarified that 'a broad impairment-related definition of disability is in line with the Convention'.[69] The Irish definition is indeed not exclusively medical; aspects of the social model of disability, on which the CRPD is based, are also evident. The inclusion of past, present, future or imputed disabilities clearly addresses social prejudice, and the lack of any requirement regarding duration may be contrasted with the CJEU's emphasis on 'long-lasting' conditions.[70] The EEA's approach is therefore more compliant with the CRPD, which states that disability 'includes' long-lasting conditions but does not limit it to these.[71] The EEA's failure to stipulate that a disability must

---

[66] *Nano Nagle School v Daly* [2018] IECA 11 (31 January 2018).

[67] See Section 2.4.

[68] Joined Cases C-335/11 and C-337/11, *HK Danmark, Acting on Behalf of Jette Ring v Dansk almennyttigt Boligselskab and HK Danmark, Acting on Behalf of Lone Skouboe Werge v Dansk Arbejdsgiverforening, Acting on Behalf of Pro Display A/S (Ring and Skouboe Werge)* [2013] ECLI:EU:C:3013: 222.

[69] UN Committee on the Rights of Persons with Disabilities 'General Comment No. 6 (2018) on equality and non-discrimination' (2018) UN Doc CRPD/C/GC/6, [73(b)].

[70] Ibid.

[71] CRPD, Art 1. There have been some difficulties in practice where tribunal decisions followed the case law of the CJEU and required disabilities to be long-term (see, for example, *Colgan v Boots Ireland Ltd* DEC–E2010-008). This is clearly erroneous, as the FED does not prevent member states from providing greater levels of protection than required under EU law.

affect a person's ability to function also contrasts favourably with the CJEU's continued emphasis on a 'limitation' arising from an impairment.[72] Overall, the Irish definition of disability clearly complies with the CRPD.

However, one significant area of non-compliance must be highlighted. While the EEA covers multiple discriminatory grounds (including race, age, gender, disability and sexual orientation, among others),[73] it does not capture intersectional discrimination. It is possible to claim multiple grounds of discrimination regarding different incidents or as alternative claims regarding the same incident. However, it is not possible to recover under multiple headings for the same incident or to claim discrimination resulting from the combined effect of different characteristics.[74] This is because s 6(1)(a) of the EEA prohibits discrimination 'on any of the grounds specified', and 'any' is taken to mean one ground only.[75] Likewise, the s 14A definition of harassment as 'unwanted conduct related to any of the discriminatory grounds' has been interpreted as relating to one ground only.[76] Although some cases have suggested an intersectional approach, closer examination indicates multiple rather than intersectional discrimination.[77]

4.5 Structural considerations: the tribunal system and legal representation

The Irish tribunal structure has undergone significant changes in recent years. Disability discrimination cases under the EEA

---

[72] See Section 2.5.

[73] EEA, s 6(2).

[74] For a discussion, see Lucy-Ann Buckley, '"Doing gender" and Irish Employment law', in Lynsey Black and Peter Dunne (eds), *Gender in Ireland: Law, Reform, Critique* (Hart Publishing 2019), 233–4.

[75] See, for example, *Maher v HSE South* DEC-E2016-144.

[76] Ibid.

[77] For a discussion, see Buckley, in note 74, 234.

were originally brought to the Equality Tribunal (ET), with an appeal to the Labour Court (LC) and a further appeal to the Circuit Court and then to the High Court on a point of law. ET cases were heard by specialist equality officers (EOs). The tribunal system was extensively overhauled in 2015,[78] and discrimination complaints are now brought to the Workplace Relations Commission (WRC), where they are heard by adjudication officers (AOs), again with an appeal to the LC and a further appeal to the High Court on a point of law. LC appeals are heard *de novo*, that is, the LC hears the case afresh, without reference to the decision of the AO.

Several systemic features must be highlighted. First, while mediation is encouraged, there is no equivalent of the Advisory, Conciliation and Arbitration Service (ACAS) early conciliation process in the UK. The WRC has a Mediation Service, as did the ET, though cases cannot be referred to mediation if either party objects.[79] While intended to promote settlement where possible and the subject of some favourable commentary,[80] the WRC Mediation Service has also been criticized for a lack of availability.[81]

Second, while neither EOs nor AOs must be legally qualified,[82] the ET was a specialist body, whose officers developed considerable expertise in the field of equality.[83] The remit of the WRC is much broader, as it replaces multiple

---

[78] Workplace Relations Act 2015.

[79] Ibid, s 39.

[80] O'Sullivan and MacMahon, in note 21, 337.

[81] Brian Barry, 'Workplace dispute resolution in Ireland at a crossroads: challenges and opportunities' (2021) 66 *The Irish Jurist*, 44, 58.

[82] The Supreme Court recently upheld this as constitutional: *Tomasz Zalewski (Applicant/Appellant) v An Adjudication Officer, the Workplace Relations Commission, Ireland and the Attorney General (Respondents)* and *Buywise Discount Store Limited (Notice Party)* [2021] IESC 29.

[83] However, a 2011 survey by Barry of over 100 representatives with expertise in employment law cases found that 60 per cent were dissatisfied with EOs: Brian Barry, 'Surveying the scene: how representatives' views

forums that previously dealt with a wide range of employment law issues. AOs are therefore not necessarily equality specialists (though some are also former EOs).

Third, while the tribunal system is informal, legal representation is common, as is representation by employer bodies or trade unions. However, costs cannot be awarded and many victims of discrimination and harassment may be unable to afford legal representation. The civil legal aid system in Ireland limits representation to specified courts or tribunals, which do not include the WRC or LC (or, previously, the ET). Effectively, therefore, legal aid is not available in most employment law complaints. Although the WRC and LC are intended to facilitate self-representation, it may be extremely difficult for lay litigants to formulate claims, prepare written submissions, make legal arguments and identify and obtain necessary proofs, particularly given the complexity of both Irish employment law and EU law, on which much Irish employment law is based. Lack of representation may thus constitute a significant barrier to both bringing claims and successful outcomes.

Fourth, Barry has highlighted a range of problems identified by practitioners and representatives in relation to the WRC. These include issues with the administration, processing and scheduling of complaints, and inconsistencies in the format of adjudication hearings, often relating to giving evidence and the availability of cross-examination.[84] Unfortunately, the Supreme Court has recently held that it is sufficient for constitutional purposes that the WRC rules allow for cross-examination where necessary (albeit at the discretion of the AO) and that this can be enforced by an action for judicial review.[85] This assumes that parties have the knowledge, time and resources

---

informed a new era in Irish workplace dispute resolution' (2018) 41 *Dublin University Law Journal*, 45, 55.

[84] Ibid, 64; Barry, in note 81, 55–8.

[85] *Zalewski*, in note 82.

to make such an application (which must be brought to the High Court). It also assumes that AOs have sufficient expertise to (generally) make appropriate decisions, even though the Supreme Court also held that they need not be legally qualified.

Finally, it should be noted that complaints before the WRC (and, previously, the ET) were, until recently, held in private. However, the Supreme Court has now held that hearings must generally be publicly accessible and decisions will no longer by anonymized.[86] It remains to be seen how this impacts discrimination claims. All LC hearings must be conducted in public unless special circumstances apply.[87]

4.6 Success rate for equality claims in Ireland

The limited Irish data on equality case outcomes suggest a low success rate, in line with the international findings previously outlined.[88] There has been no systemic analysis of Irish case law relating to disability harassment or harassment law generally. The most detailed study of Irish equality case outcomes was conducted by O'Sullivan and MacMahon, though their findings relate to the decisions of the ET and are now dated.[89] Reviewing 434 decisions under the EEA made between 2001 and 2007, O'Sullivan and MacMahon found that 65 per cent of complainants lost their cases outright and another 11 per cent were only partly successful.[90] Their analysis revealed that claims were more likely to fail or partly fail where they related to multiple discriminatory grounds. Claims relating to both discrimination and victimization might also result in partial

---

[86] Ibid. However, cases may be held in private where the AO is satisfied that special circumstances apply.

[87] Workplace Relations Act 2015, s 44. A desire for privacy does not constitute a special circumstance: *Hennessy v Crowe* UD812/2013.

[88] See Section 3.3.

[89] O'Sullivan and MacMahon, in note 21, 354.

[90] Ibid, 347.

failure (for example, a victimization claim might be upheld but not the discrimination claim).[91]

These findings are borne out by ET annual reports, which indicate that one third to half of discrimination claims across all discriminatory grounds were upheld.[92] However, the WRC annual reports are silent on this. By contrast, a recent report by the National Disability Authority found that 60 per cent of claims for reasonable accommodation (adjustment) were upheld.[93] However, this was a sample only, and there is no indication that other disability discrimination claims are as successful. It should also be noted that this comparatively high success rate resulted primarily from issue-specific procedural

---

[91] Ibid.

[92] In 2006, 44 per cent of ET decisions in relation to employment equality and pensions, across all grounds of discrimination, were pro-complainant. The Employment Appeals Tribunal, *The Employment Appeals Tribunal Thirty-Ninth Annual Report 2006* (WRC 2006), 10, www.workplacere lations.ie/en/publications_forms/corporate_matters/archived_publi cations/eat_annual_report_2006.pdf (accessed 16 January 2022). This fell to 31 per cent in 2014, the most recent year for which we have figures. The Employment Appeals Tribunal, *Annual Report 2014* (WRC 2014), 8, www.workplacerelations.ie/en/publications_forms/eat_47th _annual_report_2014.pdf (accessed 16 January 2022). The WRC does not give figures in relation to outcomes, but a chart in a recent review document indicates a success rate in the region of 25 per cent for adjudicated claims under the EEA. WRC, *Review of WRC Adjudication Decisions and Recommendations January–December 2020* (WRC 2020), 10, www.workplacerelations.ie/en/complaints_disputes/adjudication/rev iew-of-wrc-adjudication-decisions-recommendations/wrc-report-rev iew-of-wrc-adjudication-decisions-and-recommendations-jan-dec-2020-.pdf (accessed 16 January 2022).

[93] National Disability Authority, *Reasonable Accommodations: Obstacles and Opportunities to the Employment of Persons with a Disability* (National Disability Authority 2019), 7, https://nda.ie/Publications/Employm ent/Employment-Publications/Reasonable-Accommodations-Obstac les-and-Opportunities-to-the-Employment-of-Persons-with-a-Disabili ty1.pdf (accessed 19 January 2022).

failures by employers.[94] Finally, while many discrimination cases are resolved at mediation,[95] mediated agreements are confidential, and we do not know how many mediated cases relate to disability discrimination or harassment, or what their outcomes are.

4.7 Conclusion

This chapter has outlined the Irish legislative framework for addressing disability harassment at work: the EEA. The legislation defines disability very broadly and offers two heads of claim for disability harassment. These are an action for harassment under s 14A and an action for disability discrimination under s 6 and/or s 8. The chapter noted the advantages and disadvantages of each. A s 14A claim requires a nexus between the conduct and the relevant discriminatory ground but does not require a comparator; it also defines harassment and sexual harassment and sets out the criteria and parameters of the action. A discrimination claim under s 6 and/or s 8 does not require a nexus with the discriminatory ground, but does require a comparator (though a hypothetical comparator may suffice). The discrimination sections do not specify the criteria for harassment, but simply require that the complainant is treated less favourably because of disability.

The chapter noted that the provisions of the EEA are fully compliant with the FED and, in some respects, exceed the FED's requirements. However, like the FED, the EEA falls short of CRPD requirements by failing to address intersectional

---

[94] Ibid, 8.

[95] In 2014, the most recent year for which figures are available, the ET issued 102 decisions in relation to employment equality and pensions. A total of 64 cases concluded with mediation agreements, while 275 cases had other outcomes (of which 213 cases were withdrawn and 26 were closed at mediation). The Employment Appeals Tribunal (2014), in note 92, 8.

discrimination. This gap is compounded by other systemic factors that fall short of CRPD requirements, such as the failure to gather disaggregated data on disability equality and harassment claims, and the failure to ensure that legal aid is available to complainants in employment law and equality cases. This may seriously undermine access to justice for persons with disabilities.

FIVE

The Irish Legal Framework in Practice

5.1 Introduction

Chapter Four outlined the Irish legislation addressing disability harassment at work: the EEA. As noted there, the EEA is fully compliant with the FED in relation to disability harassment and meets most of the CRPD's requirements (the principal exception being its failure to address intersectional discrimination). This chapter explores the effectiveness of the EEA in addressing disability harassment at work.

The chapter focuses primarily on Allott's concept of curative effectiveness, that is, the extent to which law offers an effective means of redress for a legal wrong.[1] Mousmouti contends that the effectiveness of legislation:

> is dependent on four main elements: the purpose of a legislative text, its substantive content and legislative expression, its overarching structure and its real-life results. Each of these elements has a distinct importance for effectiveness: purpose sets the benchmark for what legislation aims to achieve; the substantive content and legislative expression determine how the law will achieve the desired results and how this will be communicated to

---

[1] Anthony Allott, 'The effectiveness of laws' (1981) 15 *Valparaiso University Law Review*, 229, 234.

its subjects; the overarching structure determines how the new provisions interact with the legal system; and real-life results of legislation indicate what has been achieved. Looking at all these elements in conjunction, the coherence and consistency offers an overall picture of the effectiveness of a legislative text and of the main problems to it.[2]

While the ultimate objective of a legal prohibition of disability harassment must be preventive, a secondary objective must be to provide effective recourse where such harassment occurs. Lack of data makes it impossible to estimate the preventive impact of the EEA, and the enforcement barriers previously outlined[3] suggest that effective recourse may be problematic. Having considered the substantive content and legislative expression of the EEA in Chapter Four, as well as the overarching structure, this chapter focuses on the operation of the EEA in practice. It does this by focusing on the outcome of specific legal cases and evaluating the redress obtained, if any.

This approach comes with many caveats. It does not follow that simply because a case was brought, a legal wrong was actually committed. Equally, it does not follow that the operation of a specific adjudication mechanism is the sole gauge by which curative effectiveness can be measured. Many employment law cases are resolved through alternative dispute resolution mechanisms, such as mediation, and legislation may also stimulate extra-legal resolution mechanisms, such as workplace grievance procedures. Legislation may also have a curative effect by shaping the form that extra-legal redress takes, as parties bargain 'in the shadow of the law'.[4] The curative effectiveness of

---

[2] Maria Mousmouti, 'Effectiveness as an aspect of quality of EU legislation: is it feasible?' (2014) 2 *The Theory and Practice of Legislation*, 309, 311.

[3] See Sections 3.2 and 4.2.

[4] Robert H. Mnookin and Lewis Kornhauser, 'Bargaining in the shadow of the law: the case of divorce' (1978) 88 *Yale Law Journal*, 950.

organizational resolution mechanisms and mediated settlements is particularly difficult to evaluate, as there is typically no publicly accessible record of such cases or their outcomes; indeed, many harassment settlements include a non–disclosure clause.[5] A focus on adjudicated outcomes therefore offers more scope for evaluation, as decisions are typically in the public domain. Even so, evaluating effectiveness is not easy, as Ireland, like most other jurisdictions, does not undertake any systemic monitoring or data gathering in relation to disability harassment cases (or indeed any other form of discrimination claim).

Evaluating case outcomes under the EEA, this chapter finds that very few disability harassment cases go to hearing and that the success rate is extremely low. The chapter then explores the reasons for the success or failure of claims, the kinds of remedies awarded, and the implications of these findings. In line with the focus of this book on intersectionality, the chapter particularly scrutinizes the decided cases for evidence of multiple and intersectional forms of discrimination, and examines the effect on case outcomes of pleading multiple discriminatory grounds. The chapter concludes with a detailed discussion of the findings, arguing that the EEA has not proved particularly effective in addressing disability harassment at work.

5.2 Methodology

The analysis in this chapter draws on intersectional theory. As outlined previously,[6] intersectionality focuses on the ways factors interact both to increase the risk of discrimination for some groups and to affect how they experience that discrimination. It recognizes that discrimination based on multiple or combined factors constitutes a distinct disadvantage, which may be both

---

[5]   Jingxi Zhai, 'Breaking the silent treatment' (2020) 2020 *Columbia Business Law Review*, 396.

[6]   See Section 1.3.

like and qualitatively different from discrimination on individual grounds.[7] Intersectional discrimination therefore differs from multiple discrimination, which refers to discrimination based on different *individual* factors, either concurrently or at different times.[8] Unlike models focusing on a single discriminatory ground, intersectionality recognizes differences in group identity and experience, and the role of power in relational structures.[9] Intersectional theory is particularly appropriate for analysing disability harassment, both because disabilities vary significantly and because disability is not the only relevant factor in every context; as noted previously,[10] gender, race and age are also significant factors affecting the frequency and form of disability harassment. This is recognized in the human rights framework, outlined in Chapter Two, and is particularly emphasized by the CRPD and the ILO Convention, both discussed in detail in that chapter.[11]

The research for this chapter employs content analysis to scrutinize all publicly available decisions on disability harassment under the EEA from 1998 to early 2020. As outlined by Hall and Wright, content analysis involves the systematic selection and analysis of a set of documents, such as judicial opinions, to record consistent features, identify common threads and draw inferences about their significance.[12] As such, 'It brings

---

[7] Kimberlé Crenshaw, 'Demarginalizing the intersection of race and sex: a black feminist critique of antidiscrimination doctrine, feminist theory and antiracist politics' (1989) *University of Chicago Legal Forum*, 139, 149.

[8] Directorate-General for Justice and Consumers (European Commission), European Network of Legal Experts in Gender Equality and Non-discrimination and Sandra Fredman, *Intersectional Discrimination in EU Gender Equality and Non-discrimination Law* (Publications Office of the European Union 2016), 27.

[9] Ibid, 30.

[10] See Section 1.3.

[11] See Sections 2.3 and 2.6.

[12] Mark A. Hall and Ronald F. Wright, 'Systematic content analysis of judicial opinions' (2008) 96 *California Law Review*, 63.

the rigor of social science to our understanding of case law, creating a distinctively legal form of empiricism.'[13] It can be used quantitatively (for example, to evaluate patterns in case outcomes) or qualitatively (for example, to identify patterns in judicial reasoning). Content analysis is most useful in evaluating decisions of equivalent value, 'where patterns across cases matter more than a deeply reflective understanding of a single pivotal case'.[14] As the objective is collective rather than individual insight, it is particularly appropriate to discrimination law, where most decisions are at the tribunal level and are routine in nature.[15]

Effective content analysis requires a consistent selection and analysis of cases, where defined elements of each are recorded and evaluated to address specific research questions.[16] This research focuses primarily on the curative effectiveness of the EEA in addressing disability harassment in the workplace, using three key indicators: (1) the number of cases going to hearing; (2) the rate of success; and (3) the remedies awarded. These indicators require some explanation and qualification.

The first key indicator (the number of cases) is inextricably entwined with preventive and facilitative effectiveness, as well as curative effectiveness. Preventive effectiveness (the degree to which particular behaviour is diminished or absent)[17] may limit instances where legal recourse is necessary, and facilitative aspects of the legal process (such as mediation) may remove the need for formal adjudication.[18] However, the number of

---

[13] Ibid, 64

[14] Ibid, 66.

[15] Alysia Blackham, 'Why do employment age discrimination cases fail? An analysis of Australian case law' (2020) 42 *Sydney Law Review*, 1, 3.

[16] Hall and Wright, in note 12, 80.

[17] Allott, in note 1, 234.

[18] Facilitative effectiveness is defined by Allott as the law 'providing formal recognition, regulation and protection for an institution of the law' (ibid). Although Allott does not expressly reference adjudication or resolution processes, they would clearly fall within the facilitative function of law.

cases going to hearing may also reflect social or institutional barriers to justice, which directly undermine the law's curative effectiveness.

The second key indicator (the rate of success) does not necessarily correlate with curative effectiveness, as it cannot be assumed that all claims going to hearing are well founded. Nevertheless, a very low success rate might indicate curative ineffectiveness, as it seems unlikely that cases are predominantly ill-founded. No attempt was made to 'second guess' case outcomes for analytical purposes.

The third key indicator (the remedies awarded) relates to curative effectiveness as it focuses on compensation for injuries. However, equality law remedies may also have a preventive function (for example, requiring employers to adopt equality policies or provide equality training) or a facilitative effect (for example, directing employers to implement appropriate complaint processes).

The key indicators are considered in the light of seven hypotheses derived from the literature and pre-existing data, as discussed in previous chapters. These are: (1) that the number of cases would not be large (given the multiple barriers that may discourage complaints); (2) that one quarter to one half of claims would be successful (based on available outcome data for discrimination claims in Ireland and limited research on harassment claims in the UK, which has quite similar legislation)[19]; (3) that multiple discrimination claims would be common and would be less successful than single-ground claims (based on intersectional discrimination research findings); (4) that sexual harassment claims would be common, especially by female complainants (also based on intersectional discrimination research findings); (5) that complainants with legal representation would be more successful (based on the complexity of equality law and the 'inequality of arms'

---

[19] Discussed in Section 6.2b.

highlighted in reports and the general literature)[20]; (6) that more cases would reference s 14A of the EEA (the specific harassment section) than s 6 or s 8 (the discrimination provisions), as it is the most obvious option and offers the most detailed protection; and (7) that most unsuccessful cases would fail due to the reasonable steps defence (based on the extensive protection otherwise provided in s 14A and the EEA's broad definition of disability).

The research reviewed all EEA cases with decisions available on the WRC website,[21] which includes ET and LC decisions, as well as WRC cases. Hall and Wright suggest that content analysis should be used with caution where some decisions have significantly more status or influence than others,[22] so the inclusion of LC decisions was considered carefully. On balance, they were included as the LC, like the WRC (and previously the ET), is a quasi-judicial body, rather than a civil court, which generally applies employment law in a relatively routine fashion. Furthermore, as appeals to the LC are heard *de novo*, they represent an independent adjudication based on full evidence.

Potential cases were identified using the search terms 'disability' AND 'harassment'. The selection criterion was that a claim of disability harassment under the EEA was pursued at hearing. However, the search terms also permitted a review of cases where any kind of harassment was alleged by an employee identified as having a disability, potentially capturing multiple or intersectional discrimination claims. The initial search returned 218 cases, but only 110 of these, dating from 2002 to January 2020,[23] satisfied the selection criterion. However, all cases were examined for potential intersectional discrimination

---

[20] See, for example Women and Equalities Committee, *Sexual Harassment in the Workplace* (HC 2017–19, 725-I), 29.

[21] Available at: www.workplacerelations.ie/en (accessed 19 January 2022).

[22] Hall and Wright, in note 12, 84.

[23] Case selection ceased on 28 February 2020.

or other relevance. This revealed a further 14 cases with some relevance to disability harassment.

The 124 cases selected for analysis were classified into three groups: successful, unsuccessful and borderline. Cases were classified as successful or unsuccessful depending on the outcome of the disability harassment complaint, irrespective of the outcome of other heads of claim. Successful cases include cases where a disability harassment complaint was partially upheld. Borderline cases include harassment cases where the basis of the alleged harassment was insufficiently clear or where a potential disability harassment case was framed otherwise (for example, as victimization). An element of subjective judgement was therefore required. This research focuses primarily on the successful and unsuccessful cases, with occasional references to borderline cases.

All cases were analysed to identify salient features, including reasons for success or failure. This again required some subjective interpretation. Adjudicators often gave multiple, overlapping reasons for their decisions, and detailed consideration was required to categorize these thematically.

The research design incorporates intersectionality in several ways. Gender, as identified in the cases, was used as a cross-cutting variable to scrutinize other findings. Other potentially relevant factors, such as race, age and sexual orientation, could not be used as analytical variables, as information was not consistently available across cases. To test the third and fourth hypotheses and evaluate potential multiple or intersectional discrimination, all cases were reviewed for allegations of sexual harassment or harassment or discrimination on grounds other than disability. This was a crude measure, as such claims were not necessarily upheld or even pursued at hearing[24]; however, it serves as a preliminary indicator. Descriptions of alleged harassment were then scrutinized to determine if the

---

[24] A detailed examination of the outcomes of other types of discrimination claims is beyond the scope of this book.

harassment could be considered intersectional. This evaluation was again necessarily subjective and often limited by reliance on adjudicators' descriptions. It must also be noted that claims may have been presented in particular ways for tactical reasons (as discussed further in Section 5.9.7).

5.3 Overview of findings

As hypothesized, the number of cases was not high. Only 110 cases involving claims of disability harassment went to hearing; over a period of 22 years, this is extremely low, and, in fact, only 17 cases were heard before 2011.[25] More surprising was the extremely low success rate. There were only five successful cases, while 105 cases were unsuccessful (see Table 5.1). The figures thus fell far short of the hypothesis that one quarter to one half of cases would succeed. Although more cases were heard by the ET than the WRC, ET cases took place over a significantly longer period (2002–17,[26] as compared with 2015–20 for the WRC). The disproportionately high number of WRC cases may reflect the significant rise in disability equality claims in recent years.[27] Only eight cases were appealed to the LC. There were slightly more female complainants (57) than male (53). Complainants had a wide range of disability types.[28]

---

[25] The highest number of cases (15) was heard in 2018. As discussed in Section 5.9.1, other cases may have been withdrawn or settled without going to hearing.

[26] This included some legacy cases after the creation of the WRC.

[27] See note 116.

[28] For the purposes of this analysis, alleged disabilities were loosely classified based on the (often limited) case descriptions into the following broad categories: physical, psychosocial, sensory, learning disability and/or neurodivergent, pregnancy-related, imputed, and unknown. Pregnancy is not a disability within the meaning of the EEA, but a pregnancy-related condition might fall within the statutory definition.

Table 5.1: Case overview

	ET	WRC	LC	Total
Successful	1	3	1	5
Unsuccessful	59	40	6	105
Borderline	5	8	1	14
Total	65	51	8	124

5.3.1 Successful cases

Successful cases were decided between January 2014 and October 2019. This was surprising, as the EEA was enacted in 1998 (though the original harassment provisions[29] were subsequently replaced).[30] All but one successful case cited s 14A (the harassment provision). The final case cited s 6 and s 8 (the equal treatment provisions) (see Table 5.2), and referred to 'discrimination' and 'harassment' interchangeably. Only one successful complainant was male. Two successful complainants identified as having psychosocial disabilities, two had physical disabilities and one had a pregnancy-related condition.

The rate of success was significantly higher in the LC (14 per cent) than in the WRC (5 per cent) or the ET (2 per cent).[31] However, this represents only one successful LC appeal. The higher rate of success in the WRC is interesting, as the ET was a more specialist body. That said, the overwhelming picture for cases going to hearing is one of failure.

---

[29] EEA, s 32 (harassment) and s 23 (sexual harassment).

[30] EEA, s 14A, partially implementing the FED.

[31] All percentages in the findings are rounded to the nearest whole number, with numbers at .5 rounded up.

Table 5.2: Statutory provisions cited in unsuccessful claims in relation to alleged harassment

Unsuccessful claims	Section 14A (post-2004)	Section 6	Section 8	Section 23 (pre-2004)	Section 32 (pre-2004)
ET	36	23	15	1	4
WRC	18	11	6	0	1
LC	3	1	1	0	0
Total	57	35	22	1	5

5.3.2 Unsuccessful cases

Unsuccessful cases were decided between December 2002 and January 2020.[32] There is some 'double counting'. One unsuccessful ET decision was reversed on appeal by the LC and is also included in the successful cases. Two unsuccessful LC cases are appeals of unsuccessful ET cases. With that caveat in mind, the gender of the unsuccessful complainants was evenly divided, with 52 male complainants and 53 female complainants. Unsuccessful complainants identified the following disabilities: physical impairments (33), learning disabilities and/or neurodivergent (seven), psychosocial disabilities (45), pregnancy-related issues (two), and sensory conditions (ten). Some complainants had more than one disability type.[33] Three unsuccessful complainants alleged that disabilities had been wrongly imputed to them, and in 16 cases the alleged disability is not identified.

---

[32] In one case, there was no detail or finding in relation to the disability harassment claim; this claim was classified as unsuccessful, as it was not explicitly upheld.

[33] Some disabilities potentially fitted within more than one of the analytical categories but were entered under a single disability type only.

Slightly over half of the unsuccessful cases referenced s 14A and many referenced s 6 and/or s 8 (see Table 5.2). Some early cases referenced the previous statutory provisions on harassment (s 32) or sexual harassment (s 23). Section references were not mutually exclusive; for example, of those citing s 14A, seven also cited s 6, and one of these additionally cited s 8. Likewise, 21 claims referenced both s 6 and s 8. Many complainants did not reference any statutory provisions, but in line with the informal nature of the tribunal, adjudicators accepted this if the general nature of the claim was clear. Often, the sole reference to legislative provisions (if any) was made by the adjudicator.

5.4 Reasons for failure

The reasons given by adjudicators for rejecting claims (see Table 5.3) required some interpretation, as they were not mutually exclusive and often overlapped. Nevertheless, it appeared that different (if related) points were being made. For instance, in *A Worker v A Government Department*, four connected reasons are given:

> In terms of complainant's complaint of harassment, [1] there was no evidence of harassment within the meaning of the Acts ... [2] I did not find any harassing remark by the complainant's manager which would fit the definition set out on the Acts. Furthermore, [3] the complainant confirmed that he never used the respondent's dignity at work policy to make a complaint, [4] so the provision (*sic*) of S. 14A(2) of the Acts avail the respondent regardless.[34]

Harassment claims may relate to a range of incidents, which may fail for different reasons (for example, some incidents

---

[34] *A Worker v A Government Department* DEC-E2016-116, [4.18] (numbers added for clarity).

Table 5.3: Reasons cited for failure of claim by adjudicating body

	ET 59 cases 2002–17	WRC 40 cases 2015–19	LC 6 cases 2012–20	Total 105 cases 2002–20
No prima facie case	23	19	4	46
Behaviour did not constitute harassment	14	11	0	25
Insufficient detail/ evidence	14	4	2	20
Lack of jurisdiction	11	9	1	21
No nexus	15	4	0	19
No disability	1	9	1	11
No notice of disability	4	4	0	8
Respondent's evidence preferred	8	1	0	9
Complainant failed to complain	3	3	0	6
Complainant did not appear	4	2	0	6
Respondent took reasonable steps	2	2	0	4
Other	1	0	0	1

are out of time and are insufficiently connected with later incidents for a time extension; other incidents are not deemed to constitute harassment or the alleged perpetrator was unaware of the complainant's disability at the time, so the harassment could not have been disability related).

It was hypothesized that the reasonable steps defence would be the most frequent reason for case failure. However, by far the most common reason cited (46 cases) was the lack of a *prima facie* case sufficient to transfer the onus of proof to the respondent. Sometimes, this was the only reason given; sometimes, a secondary reason was identified (such as a lack of evidence or a lack of awareness by the alleged perpetrator of the complainant's disability).[35]

In 25 cases, the conduct was held not to constitute harassment. Sometimes, this was simply a statement that the behaviour did not contravene the EEA: in *Sally Dowling v Debenhams Plc*, the AO commented: 'There is no evidence of unwanted conduct that violate [sic] a person's dignity or the creation of a degrading environment.'[36] In *Maher v HSE South*, the EO stated: 'I am not satisfied that any of the behaviour identified by the complainant as amounting to harassment of her is encompassed by the definition of harassment in the statute'.[37] Quite often, the adjudicator believed the behaviour did not constitute harassment because it could be otherwise interpreted[38] or had a non-discriminatory explanation. In *A Worker v A Restaurant*, the EO commented:

> he alleged that Ms B harassed him in so far as she kicked him, touched him inappropriately and shouted at him. It is clear that Ms B did regularly touch him, including with her foot, and spoke loudly to him. It is also clear that she did so because he was hard of hearing and the complainant himself had requested that she communicate with him in this manner.[39]

---

[35] See, for example, *A Nurse v A Hospital* ADJ-00000278.

[36] *Sally Dowling v Debenhams Plc* DEC-E2017-085.

[37] *Maher v HSE South* DEC-E2016-144.

[38] See, for example, *Mr A v An Employer* DEC-E2010-075.

[39] *A Worker v A Restaurant* DEC-E2012-161, [5.6].

Sometimes, the alleged harassment was regarded as normal business behaviour. In *A Clerical Officer v A Public Service Employer*, it was said that 'normal oversight of the complainant could not be described as harassment or discriminatory'.[40] In *A Software Engineer v A Respondent*, subjecting the complainant to a performance review did not amount to harassment, particularly as other employees were also reviewed and the complainant admitted his performance was in question.[41] In *A Retail Manager v A Supermarket Chain*, the AO held that a dispute over contractual terms could not be described as 'harassment'.[42]

The related reason of 'lack of nexus', identified in 19 cases, is different. The previous point was that the behaviour did not amount to harassment because it did not undermine the complainant's dignity at work or was not discriminatory. However, behaviour that was unwanted, intimidating and humiliating might still not constitute harassment if it lacked a clear 'nexus' with the complainant's disability. As the EO in one case stated:

> For a complaint of discrimination under the Employment Equality Acts to be made out, it must be demonstrated that there is a nexus between the alleged discriminatory treatment and the discriminatory grounds, for example disability. The provisions of the Employment Equality Acts, in particular those relating to harassment, do not create a 'general civility code' for the workplace.[43]

Likewise, in *Mr L v A Manufacturing Company*, the EO commented: 'No doubt being taunted in the manner alleged

---

[40] *A Clerical Officer v A Public Service Employer* ADJ-00018924.

[41] *A Software Engineer v A Respondent* DEC-E2012-195, [5.18].

[42] *A Retail Manager v A Supermarket Chain* ADJ-00005949.

[43] *A Customer Care Representative v A Provider of Outsourced Customer Support to a Mobile Phone Operator* DEC-E2016-092, [4.10].

could be very unpleasant, but the complainant did not adduce any evidence that the conduct was in any way connected with his disability.'[44]

It appears therefore that harassment under s 14A must be 'expressly related to the protected grounds'.[45] This might include pejorative language but could also include gestures or the circulation of recordings or images. However, lack of nexus was also cited in seven cases taken under s 6, even though the essence of a s 6 claim is comparison (less favourable treatment), rather than the inherent connection of the unwelcome behaviour to a discriminatory ground. While two of these cases also referenced s 14A, the other five did not.

A total of 20 cases failed due to insufficient evidence. Again, the finding was often quite basic, for example: 'I find the Complainant has not provided any evidence to show he was harassed.'[46] In *Bradford v Public Appointments Service*, the EO commented that the complainant 'alleges that no action was taken despite her numerous complaints. I note that the complainant has provided no evidence to support this contention. Furthermore, I have been provided with no evidence of the numerous complaints she is alleged to have made.'[47] The EO therefore questioned the complainant's credibility. Sometimes, no evidence at all was adduced to support the claim[48]; at others, the allegations lacked sufficient detail. In one case, the EO commented that the complainant 'can provide no further details as regards dates, times etc. of these interactions'.[49] In another, the evidence was 'very

---

[44] *Mr L v A Manufacturing Company* DEC-E2005-054, [4.5].

[45] *Ms Josephine Riney v Donegal ETB, Formerly Co. Donegal VEC* DEC- E2015-139.

[46] *An Electrical Engineer v An Electricity Company* ADJ-00016282.

[47] *Ms Karen Bradford v Public Appointments Service* DEC-E2007-02, [5.3].

[48] *Ilona Latvenaite v Rocliffe Ltd and ABP (Anglo Beef Processors Ireland t/a ABP)* DEC-E2014-038, [6.61].

[49] *Sacha v Seaview Hotel Ltd* DEC-E2016-055.

generic' and did not include 'details of specific incidents'.[50] In a case where the complainant had a 'long-term slow-learning disability', the EO stated: 'The complainant was not in a position to expand on the language or manner used by this colleague and, as such, has not established facts from which harassment, in terms of the Acts, can be inferred.'[51] It is unclear if the complainant's disability contributed to this lack of detailed evidence; if so, it highlights a barrier that may be experienced by employees with intellectual disabilities.

A total of 21 cases failed due to a lack of jurisdiction. This almost always referred to the expiry of the limitation period (normally six months), but in a few cases, complainants had signed waivers or a statutory exclusion applied. Delay could have catastrophic effects: in one case, the evidence of harassment was uncontested, but the claim was out of time and could not be upheld.[52] The failure of these claims was not always due to a lack of legal advice, for example, in five cases where a time extension might have helped, no such application was made, even though the complainant had legal representation.

Despite the very broad definition of disability in the EEA, 11 cases failed because the complainant was held not to have had a disability at the relevant time.[53] The issue was sometimes one of timing, for example, the complainant's disability developed after the alleged harassment. Some complainants failed to provide evidence of their disability[54]; in other cases, the complainant's condition (such as workplace stress,[55] backache[56]

---

[50] *Food and Beverage Assistant v A Hotel* ADJ-00012892.

[51] *A Complainant v A Private Security Firm* DEC-E2011-231, [4.8].

[52] *A Worker v An Employer* DEC-E2012-132.

[53] See, for example, *Mullen v Smurfit Kappa Ireland Limited* DEC-E2012-176.

[54] For example, *An Employee v A Government Department* ADJ-00015888.

[55] *A Training Co-ordinator/Instructor v A Training and Rehabilitation Organisation* ADJ-00017677.

[56] *Maher v HSE South* DEC-E2016-144.

or pregnancy[57]) was held not to constitute a disability. One complainant felt that she had been mocked about her ears, which she considered to be unusually protruding; the EO noted that the complainant had never sought medical advice regarding her ears and considered that the alleged protrusion was not noticeable enough to constitute a disfigurement, hence there was no disability or imputed disability.[58]

Some complainants failed to notify their employers regarding their disabilities, often due to sensitivities about the conditions in question. However, where an employer or perpetrator was unaware of the complainant's disability, it followed that they could not have harassed the complainant on this basis.[59] Some complainants argued unsuccessfully that the respondent was on notice of their disability. In one case, informing her supervisor that she was taking a course on mindfulness was held not to put the employer on notice of the complainant's disability[60]; in another, indicating that she had difficulties reading and writing did not put the employer on notice of a disability, as there might have been other reasons for this.[61]

In nine cases, the adjudicator expressly preferred the respondent's evidence. Sometimes, this reflected a lack of corroboration for the complainant's version of events.[62] In other cases, there was simply a statement of preference, such as: 'Overall, given the sequence of events in this case, I prefer the evidence of the supervisor and the testimony of the witnesses presented on behalf of the respondent.'[63]

---

[57] *Food and Beverage Assistant v A Hotel* ADJ-00012892.

[58] *Roksana Wypch v Pagewell Concessions (Ilac) Ltd Trading as Euro 50 Store, Ilac Centre* DEC-E2015-080.

[59] See, for example, *Ms A v A Charitable Organisation* DEC-E2011-049.

[60] *An Employee v A Healthcare Company* ADJ-00017070.

[61] *A Complainant v A Food Processing Company Limited* DEC-E2012-064.

[62] *Sacha v Seaview Hotel Ltd* DEC-E2016-055, [5.11].

[63] *A Complainant v A Named Development Association & FÁS* DEC-E2013-057, [4.6].

In six cases, the adjudicator highlighted the complainant's failure to report the harassment to the employer or to avail of internal complaint mechanisms.[64] The rationale for this was given in *Conlon v Intel Ireland Ltd*, where the EO stated:

> Whilst the Acts attach liability to an employer for the behaviour of its employees, it seems self-evident that before any such liability is fully fixed, the respondent is afforded an opportunity to remedy the situation. In order to do so it must be advised or at least have some knowledge of the impugned behaviour. ... I find it unreasonable for the complainant to make a conscious decision not to report the impugned behaviour to the respondent in accordance with the internal Policy and seek remedy elsewhere.[65]

Failure to complain was linked with the respondent's ability to avail of the reasonable steps defence, which was cited in only four cases. In *A Complainant v A Third Level Institution*, the EO stated:

> I am satisfied that the respondent had a harassment policy which, in all the circumstances of the present complaint, was adequate enough to provide the complainant with recourse to make a harassment complaint and to meet the requirements of Section 14A in that respect. She failed to make a complaint under that policy. It is not enough for her to say she did not trust the respondent in that context. ... In that context, the respondent is entitled to rely on the defence available in Section 14A.[66]

---

[64] See, for example, *Josef Walkowaik v O'Leary International Limited* DEC-E2016-022, [4.9].

[65] *Conlon v Intel Ireland Ltd* DEC-E2014-100, [5.20].

[66] *A Complainant v A Third Level Institution* DEC-E2012-160, [5.24].

A few other reasons for failure also arose. In six cases, the complainant simply did not appear at the hearing; in another, the complainant's credibility was affected by his acknowledgement that he had lied about various work-related matters, though all claims also failed on the facts.[67] Finally, while most reasons for failure applied reasonably equally to men and women, almost all complainants who were held not to have a disability or not to have notified the employer regarding their disability were women.[68]

5.5 Reasons for success

Reasons cited for successful outcomes (see Table 5.4) are often simply mirror images of the reasons cited for case failure: the existence of a *prima facie* case; the nature of the behaviour; the quality or quantity of the evidence; and policy and procedural failings by employers. Most cases cited several reasons for success, which were often interlinked, for example, a preference for the complainant's evidence meant that she had established a *prima facie* case.[69]

Regarding evidence, typical comments included finding the complainant's evidence 'persuasive'[70] or 'very credible'.[71] In *Kristina Blumberga v Kilbush Nurseries Ltd*, the EO noted of the complainant's evidence that 'Almost everything she said could be verified by documentary evidence e.g. medical certificates, text messages kept and references from employers after her employment for the respondent was terminated. In

---

[67] *A Complainant v A Respondent* DEC-E2013-128.

[68] 'No disability' applied to ten women and one man. 'No notice of disability' applied to seven women and one man. A few other gender differences arose: preference for the respondent's evidence applied to more men than women (six men and three women), as did the 'no nexus' ground (12 men and seven women). Some reasons for failure were cited too infrequently to regard differences as noteworthy.

[69] *Kristina Blumberga v Kilbush Nurseries Ltd* DEC-E2015-165, [4.9].

[70] *An Employee v An Employer* DEC-E2016-005.

[71] *A Security Guard v A Security Firm* ADJ-00018217.

Table 5.4: Reasons cited for success of claim

	ET	WRC	LC	Total
Complainant's evidence preferred	1	2	1	4
Prima facie case	1	2	0	3
Behaviour constituted harassment	0	2	1	3
Clear nexus with disability	0	1	1	2
Respondent's evidence inadequate	0	2	0	2
No harassment policy	1	1	0	2
Inadequate investigation	0	2	0	2
Respondent cannot rely on statutory defence	0	1	0	1

contrast, the respondent had no contemporaneous notes to corroborate their version of events.'[72] The EO added that 'One of the reasons that the complainant's evidence was credible was that she was frank about things that occurred that did not assist her case.'[73] In other cases, the complainant's evidence was not contested in direct evidence[74] or due to the absence of a key witness.[75]

Lack of evidence from the respondent sometimes overlapped with other reasons, such as policy or procedural gaps. In *An Employee v An Employer*, the EO noted that 'The Respondent did not produce evidence of an equality policy or a policy specifically dealing with harassment' and 'provided no evidence of having investigated the complaint made by the Complainant's solicitors on her behalf'.[76] In other cases, the

---

[72] *Kristina Blumberga v Kilbush Nurseries Ltd* DEC-E2015-165, [4.4].

[73] Ibid, [4.9].

[74] *Sea and Shore Safety Services Ltd v Amanda Byrne* EDA143.

[75] *A Security Guard v A Security Firm* ADJ-00018217.

[76] *An Employee v An Employer* DEC-E2016-005, [4.2].

adjudicator simply noted the lack of a relevant policy[77] or that an employer had failed to take reasonably practicable steps to address the complaint,[78] so that the statutory defence did not apply. In one case, the EO noted that the respondent had entered discussions to try to resolve the matter informally but held that while this put the investigation on hold, it 'did not remove the obligation on the employer to conduct an investigation should this alternative not be successful'.[79]

The behaviour held to constitute disability harassment was quite varied and included spoken words, gestures, the circulation of video recordings of the complainant for staff 'merriment'[80] and being sidelined and excluded at work. Three cases made clear statements about the nature of the harassment, identifying it as humiliating, offensive or intimidating. In *An Employee v A Chain of Retail Stores*, the AO stated that the complainant's 'basic right, and that of any employee, able or disabled, to the provision of dignity at work was seriously undermined'.[81] In *A Security Guard v A Security Firm*, the AO commented that 'this incident of inappropriate, offensive and unwelcome behaviour … had the effect of violating the Complainant's dignity and subjecting him to a hostile and intimidating workplace'.[82]

Two cases found a nexus between the form of the harassment and the complainant's disability. In *Sea and Shore Safety Services Ltd v Amanda Byrne*, the complainant, who had a rat phobia, alleged that the perpetrator had 'shouted, screamed and raised his voice to her regarding the smell of dead rodents' and had referred to the rats infesting the premises as her 'little friends'.[83]

---

[77] *Kristina Blumberga v Kilbush Nurseries Ltd* DEC-E2015-165, [4.9].

[78] *A Security Guard v A Security Firm* ADJ-00018217.

[79] *An Employee v An Employer* DEC-E2016-005, [4.2].

[80] *An Employee v A Chain of Retail Stores* ADJ-00003084.

[81] Ibid.

[82] *A Security Guard v A Security Firm* ADJ-00018217.

[83] *Sea and Shore Safety Services Ltd v Amanda Byrne* EDA143.

The LC noted that the resulting hostile environment was clearly connected with the complainant's disability.[84] In *A Security Guard v A Security Firm*, the AO considered that the language used in shouting at the complainant 'was clearly a reference to the Complainant's mental health issues and was therefore directly linked to his disability'.[85] However, a second incident, which also involved 'totally inappropriate' language and that 'had the effect of subjecting [the complainant] to further hostility and intimidation in the workplace', was held not to constitute harassment due to the lack of 'any nexus between the inappropriate behaviour ... and the Complainant's disability'.[86] By contrast, one case held that a sufficient connection between the *reason* for the behaviour and the disability could also suffice. There, the EO held that changes to the complainant's work pattern constituted harassment, as they were inextricably linked to her absence on medical leave.[87] This seems contrary to the approach in other decisions based on s 14A[88] and suggests a broader approach. This is bolstered by the reasoning of the EO in *A Complainant v A Third Level Institution*,[89] discussed later.

Some unsuccessful cases also illustrate behaviour amounting to disability harassment, even though the claims ultimately failed. In *Conlon v Intel Ireland Ltd*,[90] the complainant alleged that he had been referred to as 'blind Andrew', which the EO noted would come within the definition of harassment. The case failed because the complainant did not avail of the employer's harassment policy, and no finding was made on the harassment point. In *A Worker v An Employer*, the complainant's employer told her that he had learned that she was taking

---

[84] Ibid.

[85] *A Security Guard v A Security Firm* ADJ-00018217.

[86] Ibid.

[87] *An Employee v An Employer* DEC-E2016-005.

[88] For example, *Harrington v Natus Nicolet Ireland Limited* DEC-E2012-197.

[89] *A Complainant v A Third Level Institution* DEC-E2012-160, [5.27].

[90] *Conlon v Intel Ireland Ltd* DEC-E2014-100.

depression medication and did not want her 'doped out of it' on the shop floor.[91] He therefore sent the complainant home and terminated her employment. The complainant's evidence was uncontested but her complaint was out of time. In *A Complainant v A Third Level Institution*, the EO accepted that an alleged 'swirling motion' by the complainant's supervisor was 'designed to denigrate the complainant with respect to her mental health'.[92] The complainant's manager also treated her in a very hostile and intimidating manner regarding her medical appointments and sick leave certificates. The EO was satisfied that the treatment was influenced by the complainant's disability and that a *prima facie* case of harassment had been established, though it failed because the complainant did not report the incidents to the respondent. However, a victimization claim was upheld, as the treatment worsened after the complainant brought proceedings.

5.6 The significance of legal representation

All but one successful case involved representation of some kind for both parties (see Table 5.5),[93] and 44 per cent of all parties had legal representation. Parties in unsuccessful cases had roughly equivalent levels of legal representation. However, respondents were much more likely than complainants to have non–legal representation (such as representatives from employer organizations), whereas complainants were more likely to self-represent, probably because legal aid is not available before the WRC or LC (or previously, the ET). The level of trade union representation was low. In some complex cases, the adjudicator noted that the complainant was urged to obtain

---

[91] *A Worker v An Employer* DEC-E2012-132, [2.6].

[92] *A Complainant v A Third Level Institution* DEC-E2012-160, [5.27].

[93] Following LC practice, the terms 'complainant' and 'respondent' are retained for the same parties throughout, irrespective of who appeals.

Table 5.5: Overall party representation

Party	Representation	Successful	Unsuccessful
Complainant	Legal	4	49
Complainant	Other	0	7
Complainant	None	1	48
Complainant	Unknown	0	1
Respondent	Legal	1	48
Respondent	Other	3	26
Respondent	None	1	30
Respondent	Unknown	0	1

representation but had not done so.[94] No explanation for this failure was noted in the decision.

With some exceptions, representation generally did not greatly affect the frequency with which particular reasons for failure were cited (see Table 5.6). Lack of jurisdiction was cited more often where the complainant did not have representation, while lack of nexus, insufficient evidence and a preference for the respondent's evidence were cited less often. The complainant's failure to complain, lack of nexus and a preference for the respondent's evidence were cited more often where the respondent had representation, while behaviour was more commonly said not to constitute harassment where the respondent did not have representation. However, it is unclear what causative relationship, if any, exists for these differences.

5.7 Intersectional harassment

It was correctly hypothesized that many cases would allege discrimination based on multiple grounds and that these would

---

[94] For example, *An IT Systems Support Officer v A Hospital* ADJ-00021831; *Food and Beverage Assistant v A Hotel* ADJ-00012892.

Table 5.6: Frequency of citation in cases where parties had or did not have legal or other representation

Reason	Complainant had representation (56 cases)	Complainant had no representation (48 cases)	Respondent had representation (74 cases)	Respondent had no representation (30 cases)
No prima facie case	43%	44%	42%	47%
Behaviour did not constitute harassment	27%	19%	20%	30%
Insufficient detail/evidence	27%	11%	20%	17%
Lack of jurisdiction	16%	23%	19%	20%
No nexus	21%	15%	20%	13%
No disability	11%	11%	9%	13%
No notice of disability	11%	4%	8%	7%
Respondent's evidence preferred	14%	2%	11%	3%
Complainant failed to complain	7%	4%	8%	0%
Complainant did not appear	2%	10%	7%	3%
Respondent took reasonable steps	5%	2%	3%	7%
Other	0%	2%	1%	0%

be less successful than single-ground claims. Successful cases generally did not involve claims on other grounds, though it is difficult to read much into this, as only five cases succeeded. For the same reason, it is difficult to comment on the impact of impairment type. However, many unsuccessful cases involved claims of discrimination (not necessarily harassment) on other grounds (see Table 5.7), though these claims were frequently not pursued at hearing. The most common additional grounds cited were race (16) and gender (22). More women than men cited gender and family status discrimination ('family status' essentially denotes caring responsibilities), but more men than women claimed marital status discrimination.

Only one successful case alleged harassment on another ground (discussed later). In some unsuccessful cases, harassment on multiple grounds was alleged (see Table 5.8), but, again, not all grounds were necessarily pursued at hearing. It was hypothesized that many female complainants would allege sexual harassment, but only two sexual harassment claims were made, and only one complainant was female. Both claims failed, though gender harassment was found in one case.[95] No claims of harassment on grounds other than disability were upheld in the unsuccessful cases.

When descriptions of harassment were analysed, three cases raised potential intersections between gender, pregnancy and disability, though only one succeeded.[96] In *Kristina Blumberga v Kilbush Nurseries Ltd*,[97] the complainant alleged harassment based on an illness or disability related to her pregnancy. The EO treated this as harassment on the grounds of gender and disability, and found that the complainant was treated differently to other pregnant workers because her pregnancy was perceived as 'difficult'.[98] However, the EO did not discuss

---

[95] *Eithne McDermott v Connacht Gold Co-operative Society Ltd* DEC-E2011-147.

[96] *Kristina Blumberga v Kilbush Nurseries Ltd* DEC-E2015-165.

[97] Ibid.

[98] Ibid.

Table 5.7: Unsuccessful claims by type of discrimination alleged

Type of discrimination alleged	Disability	Race	Gender	Marital status	Sexual orientation	Family status	Age
Female complainants (53)	53	7	16	3	2	7	3
Male complainants (52)	52	9	6	6	3	1	4
Total complainants	105	16	22	9	5	8	7

Table 5.8: Unsuccessful claims by type of harassment alleged

Type of harassment alleged	Disability harassment only	More than one type of harassment	Sexual harassment
Female complainants	33	20	1
Male complainants	37	15	1
Total complainants	70	35	2

whether the complainant had a disability within the meaning of the EEA. The harassment involved telling the complainant, 'Next time keep your legs closed' – a remark that does not have an obvious disability nexus, but was made in the context of the complainant's pregnancy-related illness. By contrast, in *Food and Beverage Assistant v A Hotel*, where the complainant alleged harassment 'on the grounds of disability due to pregnancy', the AO held that 'pregnancy does not constitute disability within the meaning of the Act'.[99] However, the complainant here gave evidence that she did not have a disability and had not informed the respondent of her health problems. In the third case, *A Complainant v A Third Level Institution*,[100] the complainant claimed that she was harassed because of her psychosocial condition, understood to be post-natal depression. Although she established a *prima facie* case of harassment (which failed due to a lack of reporting), the EO considered that the harassment did not relate to her current pregnancy, but rather only to her disability, which was connected with a previous pregnancy. The EO stated that this aspect of the complainant's disability was 'only a part, perhaps even a small part, of her

---

[99] *Food and Beverage Assistant v A Hotel* ADJ-00012892.
[100] *A Complainant v A Third Level Institution* DEC-E2012-160.

overall mental health issues'[101] and could not be considered part of her pregnancy.

A potential example of intersectional harassment occurred in a borderline case, *Ms Bridget Connolly v Health Service Executive*, where the complainant alleged that she had been referred to as a 'neurotic old lady'.[102] Although the complaint only alleged age discrimination, it represented a potential intersection of age and disability discrimination (where older women might be denigrated as particularly prone to neurosis). The case echoes an early ET decision (not examined for this research), where a young female manager was referred to repeatedly by an older male colleague as 'only a young fooling girl more inexperienced than he'.[103] This was held to constitute harassment connected with the complainant's age and sex, though presumably on a multiple discrimination basis given the inability of the EEA to address intersectional claims. In *Connolly*, the complaint was out of time and could not be investigated further.

The best example of potentially intersectional harassment (though no such claim was made) occurred in another borderline case, *Hannon v First Direct Logistics Limited*.[104] The complainant was transgender and was diagnosed with gender identity disorder. She was, among other things, asked to present as male for particular periods and purposes (including seeing clients), called by her previous male name, denied an email address in her new name, and forbidden to use the female toilets. She was also asked to work from home and told that her presence in the office caused a bad atmosphere. She successfully claimed both gender and disability discrimination on different points, but much of the

---

[101] Ibid, [5.22].

[102] *Ms Bridget Connolly v Health Service Executive* DEC-E2008-061.

[103] *A Complainant v A Company* DEC-E2002-014.

[104] *Hannon v First Direct Logistics Limited* DEC-E2011-066.

treatment she received could have grounded a harassment claim, as it undermined her dignity and resulted in a hostile working environment.[105] The harassment was not related to gender alone, as the complainant's gender, dress, name and conduct were inextricably linked to her diagnosed medical condition, which both parties had accepted amounted to a disability.

5.8 Remedies

Compensation for disability harassment in the few successful cases ranged from €7,500[106] to €62,000.[107] However, not all awards were disaggregated where complainants succeeded under multiple headings. Non-financial remedies were also awarded in two cases. In one, the EO directed the respondent to prepare a comprehensive equality policy, including appropriate complaint procedures, and to ensure all staff were adequately trained in this.[108] In the other, the AO directed that all staff with management functions should be trained in the respondent's bullying and harassment policy, and that training should be kept under review in light of best practice.[109]

5.9 Discussion

The discussion first addresses points arising from the key indicators, followed by issues connected with the additional hypotheses.

---

[105] This is implicit in the decision of the EO (*Hannon v First Direct Logistics Limited* DEC-E2011-066, [4.8]).

[106] *An Employee v A Chain of Retail Stores* ADJ-00003084.

[107] *An Employee v An Employer* DEC-E2016-005.

[108] Ibid.

[109] *A Security Guard v A Security Firm* ADJ-00018217.

5.9.1 The low number of cases going to hearing

The low number of cases does not seem reflective of either the broad legislative protection or the available data on disability-related discrimination in Ireland. However, this is unlikely to represent the complete story, as it is highly likely that many cases may settle. Although conciliation is not mandatory in Ireland, there is nevertheless a good proportion of mediated outcomes in equality cases generally,[110] though we do not know how many of these relate to disability harassment. There may also be non-mediated settlements, though we have no information on these. The statutory code of practice[111] may also have increased good practice and encouraged local dispute resolution; again, we have no information on the level of disability harassment complaints in particular businesses or sectors, including the public sector.[112] In their review of Irish employment equality cases, O'Sullivan and MacMahon suggest that settlement may be the hope from the outset in some cases;[113] they also suggest that many complainants may settle, withdraw their claim or simply abandon the process once they realize how long it can take.[114] Without external monitoring and more extensive research, we simply do not know.

---

[110] See Section 4.5.

[111] Irish Human Rights and Equality Commission, 'Code of practice on sexual harassment and harassment at work' (2022). Previous codes of practice were adopted in 2002 and 2012.

[112] Reporting obligations have recently been implemented in relation to higher education institutions in Ireland. Carl O'Brien, 'Colleges must report annual bullying and sexual harassment figures' (2020) *The Irish Times*, 26 November, www.irishtimes.com/news/education/colleges-must-report-annual-bullying-and-sexual-harassment-figures-1.4420156 (accessed 19 January 2022).

[113] Michelle O'Sullivan and Juliet MacMahon, 'Employment equality legislation in Ireland: claimants, representation and outcomes' (2010) 39 Industrial Law Journal 329, 338.

[114] Ibid.

Alternatively, however, many employees with disabilities may simply fail to make legal complaints regarding work-related harassment. A general reluctance to take legal action is supported by the international data and literature, as well as by the low level of disability discrimination claims generally in Ireland.[115] While disability discrimination claims in Ireland have risen significantly in recent years,[116] they are still extremely low considering that there are over 176,000 persons with disabilities in the labour market.[117] It is interesting to recall O'Sullivan and MacMahon's suggestion that requiring written submissions can deter some marginalized complainants, including those with certain disabilities.[118] The low number of cases may thus suggest barriers undermining the curative effectiveness of the legislation, which may prove extremely difficult to address.

5.9.2 The low success rate

It was hypothesized that one quarter to one half of cases would succeed at hearing, but less than 5 per cent did. This

---

[115] See Section 4.2.

[116] A total of 54 disability cases were referred to the ET in 2006 in relation to employment equality and pensions. The Employment Appeals Tribunal, *The Employment Appeals Tribunal Thirty-Ninth Annual Report 2006* (WRC 2006), 9, www.workplacerelations.ie/en/publications_forms/corporate_matters/archived_publications/eat_annual_report_2006.pdf (accessed 16 January 2022). This rose to 116 in 2014: The Employment Appeals Tribunal, *Annual Report 2014* (WRC 2014), 7, www.workplacerelations.ie/en/publications_forms/eat_47th_annual_report_2014.pdf (accessed 16 January 2022). There were 329 referrals to the WRC in 2019, dropping to 290 in 2020. WRC, *Workplace Relations Commission Annual Report 2019* (WRC 2019), 25, www.workplacerelations.ie/en/publications_forms/corporate_matters/annual_reports_reviews/annual-report-2019.pdf (accessed 16 January 2022).

[117] CSO, *Census 2016 Reports* (CSO 2016) www.cso.ie/en/csolatestnews/presspages/2017/census2016summaryresults-part1/ (accessed 20 September 2020).

[118] O'Sullivan and MacMahon, in note 113, 338.

is very significantly lower than the overall success rate for discrimination claims in Ireland previously outlined,[119] as well as the (apparent) success rate for harassment claims generally in the UK.[120] It is particularly surprising given the broad definition of disability in the EEA and the purely subjective test for harassment, which should make it easier to succeed in a disability harassment action in Ireland.[121] While Weber identified a very low rate of success in disability harassment claims in the US, that was in the context of very different legal standards, particularly the 'unrealistically extreme' requirement that the harassment should be 'severe and pervasive'.[122] In Ireland, by contrast, there is no such requirement, and a single incident may constitute unlawful harassment, subject to other criteria being met.[123]

While complaints may, of course, be unfounded, and many strong cases may successfully settle,[124] it seems unlikely that harassment cases going to hearing are significantly weaker than other equality cases with a significantly higher success rate. The extremely low success rate may therefore suggest that the legislative approach is problematic. However, this must be considered in light of the reasons for case failure. These largely related to the degree and quality of the supporting evidence, the nature of the behaviour, failure to demonstrate that the complainant had a disability at the relevant time, and procedural failures, such as failing to complain, engage with internal processes or adhere to statutory time limits. Some of these issues might potentially be addressed with proper advice, which could be provided through legal advisors, trade unions,

---

[119] See Section 4.6.

[120] See Section 3.3.

[121] For a discussion of the equivalent UK law, see Section 6.2.2.

[122] Mark C. Weber, *Disability Harassment* (New York University Press 2007), 26.

[123] See Section 4.3.

[124] Blackham, in note 15, 2.

statutory bodies or other mechanisms. Such advice might address whether behaviour potentially amounts to harassment, the evidence needed to support a claim (including keeping detailed records and providing medical evidence to establish a disability) or the need to inform and engage with the employer, including participating in internal processes. Some caution is required here, as the research findings do not indicate a clear correlation between representation at hearing (and whatever advice was offered prior to that) and addressing the reasons for case failure. On the other hand, we do not know what the outcome would have been without whatever advice was given, and respondents may also have received helpful advice. The research did find that 'lack of jurisdiction' was cited more often where the complainant lacked representation, suggesting that advice on time limits and extensions may have some effect. However, a more fundamental issue is whether the statutory time limit is fit for purpose. Six months is a very short time to initiate proceedings, particularly where it must also accommodate potentially protracted internal complaints mechanisms.[125] While it may be possible to apply for a time extension, the findings here suggest that this is not always done, even where complainants have legal representation.

It is also worth highlighting the impact of the burden of proof. As required by EU law, the EEA provides that where a complainant shows facts raising an inference of discrimination, the burden shifts to the employer to show that discrimination has not occurred.[126] This provision is intended to support complainants by helping them to address situations where discriminatory intent might be difficult to establish. In practice, however, it means that complainants must demonstrate a prima facie case of discrimination before an onus shifts to

---

[125] O'Sullivan and MacMahon also suggest that it may take time for someone to realize they have been harassed or discriminated against: O'Sullivan and MacMahon, in note 113, 349.

[126] EEA, s 85A.

the employer. In the cases examined here, complainants were held not to have demonstrated a prima facie case in 46 cases (43 per cent of unsuccessful cases). As noted earlier, levels of representation did not appear to affect this.

5.9.3 The range of remedies

The tiny number of successful cases makes it difficult to evaluate remedial effectiveness. Compensation varied considerably, though it was sometimes unclear how much related to harassment. O'Sullivan and MacMahon previously found that compensation awards by the ET were generally not high and were usually well below the statutory maximum, though award averages for some years were inflated by outlier cases.[127] A recent report by the WRC found that the average award under the EEA in 2020 was just under €20,000.[128]

As only five disability harassment cases examined here succeeded at hearing, two cases with non-financial orders is arguably a significant proportion. However, this may not be scalable. O'Sullivan and MacMahon found that financial compensation and awards for the loss of earnings were the most common forms of remedy awarded between 2001 and 2007, but they also found that the ET made non-financial orders in many cases. These included orders for employers to introduce or review equality policies, to improve procedures for selection or promotion, and to provide equality-related training.[129] These earlier findings suggest that the non-financial orders

---

[127] O'Sullivan and MacMahon, in note 113, 350.

[128] WRC, *Review of WRC Adjudication Decisions and Recommendations January–December 2020* (WRC 2020), 37, www.workplacerelations. ie/en/complaints_disputes/adjudication/review-of-wrc-adjudicat ion-decisions-recommendations/wrc-report-review-of-wrc-adjudicat ion-decisions-and-recommendations-jan-dec-2020-.pdf (accessed 16 January 2022).

[129] O'Sullivan and MacMahon, in note 113, 350.

identified in the current research are not outliers and may demonstrate a consistent practice across equality cases, though further research is needed to review this trend in current equality cases. The sole year for which we have current data is 2020, when the WRC directed or recommended 181 'courses of action'.[130] However, it appears that the vast majority of these did not relate to the EEA, and the number of instances related to the EEA may be as low as 18,[131] compared with 58 monetary awards.[132] That said, it is worth emphasizing that the non-financial orders made in the cases reviewed here were directed at improving structural equality, rather than the complainant's personal situation, while the instances identified in the WRC report also mostly addressed policy and training.[133] This shows a potential for systemic change, though it is, of course, unknown what impact these orders had in practice.

5.9.4 Significance of representation

It was hypothesized that complainants with legal representation would be more successful, impacting the legislation's effectiveness. While almost all successful complainants had legal representation, the low number of successful cases makes it difficult to identify this as decisive, particularly as nearly half of unsuccessful complainants also had legal representation. However, while legal representation levels for complainants and respondents were roughly equivalent, significant differences in non-legal representation may have favoured respondents. Lack of representation may also have affected the number of cases brought: adjudicators offered significant latitude to litigants in person, but legal complexity may deter many potential complainants. Surprisingly, some reasons for failure

---

[130] WRC, in note 128, 38.

[131] Ibid, 53–4.

[132] Ibid, 23.

[133] Ibid, 53–4.

were more likely to be cited in cases where complainants had representation. Some of these issues (such as a preference for the respondent's evidence) were outside complainants' control, but such issues as insufficient evidence or detail might reasonably have been identified and addressed. This may partly depend on when representation was obtained, but no information on this point was available.

Notably, 45 per cent of complainants had no representation (legal or otherwise) at hearing.[134] This is reasonably consistent with the finding of O'Sullivan and MacMahon that 36 per cent of complainants before the ET between 2001–07 were not represented and that the proportion of complainants without representation had generally increased over that period.[135] However, O'Sullivan and MacMahon found that 49 per cent of complainants with representation had trade union representation, while only 30 per cent had private legal representation.[136] By contrast, 88 per cent of complainants identified in the current research as having representation had legal representation. This suggests a very significant increase in the juridification of equality claims, though O'Sullivan and MacMahon note other findings indicating that the proportion of complainants with legal representation before other tribunals was significantly higher than in the ET.[137] The suggestion of increased juridification receives support from recent WRC data, which indicate that 47 per cent of all parties in 2020 had representation of some kind, while 53 per cent did not.[138] However, the WRC data are not disaggregated by legislative enactment.

---

[134] Where representation could be established; this was unknown in one case.

[135] O'Sullivan and MacMahon, in note 113, 343.

[136] Ibid, 343. They also note that 18 per cent of complainants in these early cases were represented by the Equality Authority, which has now been replaced by the Irish Human Rights and Equality Commission.

[137] Ibid, 343.

[138] WRC, in note 128, 12.

Almost half of all parties in the WRC report had legal representation,[139] which is slightly higher than in the current research (44 per cent), but complainants and respondents had similar rates of legal representation,[140] as in the current findings. Just under 15 per cent of complainants were represented by trade unions.[141] Overall, the WRC report tends to confirm the main trend identified in the current research, namely, that respondents are more likely than complainants to have representation, as well as to have non-legal representation, while complainants are more likely to self-represent.[142]

An ET representative cited in O'Sullivan and MacMahon's research considered that the type of representation did not affect case outcomes and noted that EOs were trained to be aware of power imbalances between parties with representation and those without.[143] Certainly, in the current research, EOs and AOs did offer considerable latitude to litigants in person, for instance, by not requiring them to ground their complaint in specific legal provisions so long as the general nature of the complaint was clear. However, O'Sullivan and MacMahon found (without commenting on causation) that plaintiffs with trade union representation were more successful than those with private legal representation and that complainants with no representation at hearing were more successful than those with private legal representation.[144] In the current research, most successful complainants had legal representation (four cases), while only one had no representation. However, less than 8 per cent of complainants with legal representation were successful overall. It is difficult to attach significance to this given the very small number of successful cases and the variety

---

[139] Ibid, 15.

[140] Ibid, 21.

[141] Ibid.

[142] Ibid.

[143] O'Sullivan and MacMahon, in note 113, 343.

[144] Ibid, 343–4.

of reasons for lack of success. Notably, in WRC cases in 2020, both complainants and respondents with representation were more successful than those without representation.[145] However, these figures were not disaggregated by legislative enactment or representation type.

5.9.5 Statutory basis for claims

It was hypothesized that most claims would reference s 14A (harassment), but a significant number of cases relied instead, or as well, on s 6 and/or s 8 (general discrimination provisions). Some complainants made no statutory references; this is understandable from lay litigants and, as noted previously, is accepted by adjudicators if the nature of the claim is clear. However, many adjudicators did not reference statutory provisions either. There was little discussion of the relevant criteria for harassment, though these may be regarded as well established. Where discussed, the greatest emphasis was on the need to demonstrate a nexus between the complainant's disability and the offending behaviour, with a few references to the subjective test for harassment and the reasonable steps defence.

As noted previously, there are advantages and disadvantages to each head of claim, which may impact on legislative efficacy. Section 14A does not require a comparator, potentially avoiding pitfalls that have dogged other equality claims. However, requiring a clear nexus between the offending conduct and the complainant's disability may fail to capture much discriminatory behaviour. Sections 6 and 8 require a comparator (actual or hypothetical) but do not require offensive behaviour to be inherently connected to the complainant's disability. It may therefore better capture some forms of targeted behaviour, assuming that an appropriate comparator can be identified.

---

[145] WRC, in note 128, 16, 18, 20.

This apparent distinction is not fully maintained in the cases analysed here. Of the 19 cases that failed due to a 'lack of nexus', five made no reference to s 14A but were based on s 6 and/or s 8. This suggests that the 'nexus' requirement is sometimes applied inappropriately. Furthermore, the issue of a comparator was not raised in any of the s 6 or s 8 cases examined. Taken together, this suggests that adjudicators may be drawing on the s 14A criteria even when referencing s 6 or s 8. Alternatively, the nexus issue may be used as a proxy for comparison, that is, a clear link between the form of the behaviour and a particular disability suggests that someone without that disability would not have been subjected to that behaviour (an implicit hypothetical comparison). These issues need to be separated, not only for doctrinal consistency, but to increase transparency, clarify what complainants must demonstrate and enhance legislative efficacy.

5.9.6 Reasonable steps defence

It was hypothesized that the main reason for case failure would be the reasonable steps defence. However, this was applied in only four cases. This was surprising, as the high level of employer representation identified in this research suggests that they are likely to be fully advised on the statutory defence and a statutory code of practice that explains the defence has been in place since 2002.[146] Cases where the defence would apply may be more likely to be resolved internally, as reasonable steps entail the implementation of appropriate harassment policies and complaints mechanisms. If so, this is an indication of the effectiveness of the legislation. However, it must also be recalled that many complaints failed due to the lack of a prima facie

---

[146] SI No. 78/2002 Employment Equality Act 1998 (Code of Practice) (Harassment) Order 2002, replaced in 2012 and again in 2022.

case. In this situation, the burden of proof does not shift to the employer, so the statutory defence does not arise.

5.9.7 Intersectional harassment and multiple discrimination

It was hypothesized that multiple discrimination claims would be common but would be less successful than single-ground claims. This proved correct insofar as harassment allegations are concerned. However, many alleged discriminatory grounds were not seriously pursued at hearing. They may initially have been cited for tactical reasons (because it is easier to drop claims than to add them), or they may have been abandoned to present cases more effectively.

Surprisingly few cases suggested intersectional harassment, as opposed to multiple discrimination. There were some cases or potential cases of intersectional harms in the transgender and pregnancy contexts. There were also some suggestions of stereotypes regarding particular groups (for example, older women). Notwithstanding the international data previously outlined,[147] there was no evidence that women with disabilities were particular targets of sexual harassment. It is possible that women with strong sexual harassment cases simply proceed under that heading, without referencing disability, even if it does not wholly reflect their experience. If so, the legislative failure to facilitate intersectional claims may be increasing the legal invisibility of intersectional forms of harassment.

The finding that multiple discrimination cases are less successful is problematic. Practically speaking, the clear advice to complainants must be to focus on one discriminatory ground only. Again, however, this is likely to increase the invisibility of intersectional forms of harassment, denying the reality of many victims' experiences and making it harder to address intersectional claims when they arise. This may reinforce

---

[147] See Section 1.4.

existing hierarchies, perpetuating disadvantage. In the short term, additional training for adjudicators and practitioners might help address these concerns, but in the long term, a proper legislative basis for intersectional claims is essential.[148]

5.10 Conclusion

This chapter has evaluated the effectiveness of the EEA in addressing work-related disability harassment, using three key indicators: the number of legal complaints going to hearing; the success rate for complaints; and the remedies awarded. In doing so, it draws on hypotheses developed from the academic literature and reported data. Many, but not all, of these hypotheses were borne out in practice. As anticipated, the number of cases was small, but the success rate fell far below expectations and proved much lower than the success rate in Irish discrimination claims generally. As expected, many cases alleged multiple discrimination, and almost none of these succeeded. There was limited evidence of intersectional forms of disability harassment, though this may be attributable to the legislative structure and to the tactical framing of claims. Complainants with legal representation were more likely to succeed than those without it, but the low number of successful cases makes it impossible to say more than that. Contrary to expectation, many cases were taken under general discrimination provisions, rather than the specific harassment section, and very few cases failed due to the reasonable steps defence. Remedies could not be analysed in detail due to the low number of successful cases, but non-financial remedies were sometimes used to address structural discrimination.

---

[148] For further analysis, see Shreya Atrey, *Intersectional Discrimination* (Oxford University Press 2019), ch 4. Atrey argues that appropriate legislative provisions are necessary but insufficient.

The chapter has identified several procedural, evidential and substantive points militating against complainant success. Procedurally, the findings indicate that the six-month limitation period for discrimination claims in Ireland is a significant obstacle in practice. Short time limits may be particularly harsh on complainants who avail of internal grievance procedures, as they may have little time left to bring a legal claim where internal complaint mechanisms prove unsuccessful. Evidential obstacles identified include the need to provide evidence of disability and reasonably detailed descriptions of alleged harassment. Many applicants, especially lay litigants, may be unaware of these requirements. Substantively, the research identified possible confusion between the operation of the harassment and general discrimination provisions, leading to the potential misapplication of the statutory criteria. Adjudicators in discrimination claims may incorrectly focus on whether conduct is inherently related to a disability, rather than on whether it demonstrates less favourable treatment.

Overall, these findings suggest that despite its apparently comprehensive provisions, the EEA does not sufficiently address the barriers that may discourage complainants or prevent access to legal complaint mechanisms, and has not proved very effective in tackling work-related disability harassment. The implications of these findings are considered further in Chapter Six.

SIX

Meeting the Global Challenge: Lessons from Experience

6.1 Introduction

This chapter considers what other jurisdictions might learn from the Irish experience and identifies a number of key lessons. First, the Irish experience raises significant concerns for the effectiveness of disability harassment legislation. The chapter therefore considers the relevance of the Irish findings to other jurisdictions, analysing key elements of the Irish legal framework from a comparative perspective. Second, the chapter examines the wider implications of the Irish findings regarding intersectional forms of harassment and argues that these are likely to remain invisible and unaddressed unless the legislative framework facilitates intersectional claims. Third, the Irish experience identifies particular barriers to legislative effectiveness, which must be addressed to combat disability harassment at work. The chapter concludes by arguing that more proactive approaches to addressing disability harassment are required and considers a positive employer duty to prevent harassment, as recently proposed in the UK and Australia.

6.2 The effectiveness of disability harassment legislation: international relevance of the Irish findings

The first lesson from the Irish experience concerns the effectiveness of disability harassment legislation in practice. The findings suggest that the Irish legislation addressing disability harassment at work, though broad in scope and largely aligning with the international legal framework, is not particularly successful in terms of either the number or the outcome of cases going to hearing. An obvious question is whether the Irish findings have an international relevance. To answer this, it is helpful to consider the Irish legislation in light of Mousmouti's framework for legislative effectiveness, outlined previously.[1] This identifies the key elements as 'the purpose of a legislative text, its substantive content and legislative expression, its overarching structure and its real-life results'.[2] Each of these elements will be considered in turn.

6.2.1 Legislative purpose

The purpose of disability harassment legislation in Ireland, deriving from the FED, is necessarily similar for other EU member states. The legislation aims to prohibit work-related discrimination (including harassment) based on disability,[3] or to provide appropriate redress where necessary,[4] in the context of achieving equality and social integration, vindicating human rights and fostering inclusion in the labour market.[5] The same overarching objectives should apply where countries have ratified the CRPD, ensuring that the purpose of the Irish legislation has a broader international relevance.

6.2.2 Substantive content and legislative expression

Even where the broad objective is the same, however, there may be significant variations in the substantive content and

---

[1] See Section 5.1.
[2] Maria Mousmouti, 'Effectiveness as an aspect of quality of EU legislation: is it feasible?' (2014) 2 *The Theory and Practice of Legislation*, 309, 311.
[3] FED, Recital 12.
[4] FED, Recital 35.
[5] FED, Recitals 1–8.

legislative expression. The impact of the FED is confined to EU member states and is not necessarily uniform in terms of legislative expression: some member states (including Ireland) draw directly on the language of the FED; others may not. The FED also informs the substantive requirements of national legislation. For instance, while the FED leaves it to member states to define harassment, it mandates that the test for harassment is subjective.[6] The national definition of disability must also satisfy the interpretation of the CJEU.[7]

A comparison with UK law demonstrates how the FED may both provide a unifying influence and allow for national variation. Although the UK is no longer an EU member state, its disability harassment legislation, contained in the Equality Act 2010 (the Equality Act), was formulated during its EU membership. The FED was therefore a key influence on the substantive content of the Equality Act and on its judicial interpretation and application. Disability harassment is covered under s 26 of the Equality Act, which has striking similarities to s 14A of the Irish EEA. The Equality Act defines harassment as 'unwanted conduct related to a relevant protected characteristic',[8] language that closely reflects the FED, as well as the EEA. As in Ireland, a single incident may constitute harassment,[9] and differential treatment related to the victim's

---

[6] Art 3 of the FED defines harassment in terms of its 'purpose or effect', making it clear that a subjective impact may suffice. For further substantive requirements see Section 2.4.

[7] Joined Cases C-335/11 and C-337/11, *HK Danmark, Acting on Behalf of Jette Ring v Dansk almennyttigt Boligselskab and HK Danmark, Acting on Behalf of Lone Skouboe Werge v Dansk Arbejdsgiverforening, Acting on Behalf of Pro Display A/S (Ring and Skouboe Werge)* [2013] ECLI:EU:C:3013: 222, [93].

[8] Equality Act, s 26(1)(a).

[9] Sam Middlemiss, '"Another nice mess you've gotten me into": employers' liability for workplace banter' (2017) 59(6) *International Journal of Law and Management*, 916, 922.

response to harassment is also covered.[10] The test for harassment in both jurisdictions is subjective, that is, whether 'the purpose or effect' of the conduct is to create a 'intimidating, hostile, degrading, humiliating or offensive environment' for the victim.[11] Again, this phrasing is taken directly from the FED. As in Ireland, a statutory defence applies where an employer takes reasonable steps to prevent harassment from occurring or to address it appropriately.[12] As in Ireland, this normally requires the adoption and implementation of a harassment policy, including an appropriate investigation process, and reversing any adverse effects of the harassment.[13]

However, there are also some differences between the legislative approaches in each jurisdiction. The EEA has no equivalent of the UK provision that the effect of conduct is to be evaluated by reference to the victim's perception, the circumstances of the case and the reasonableness of the effect.[14] Unlike the EEA, the Equality Act does not currently capture third-party harassment,[15] though it appears that this may change.[16] While the Equality Act, like the EEA, captures past, present, future or imputed (perceived) disabilities, the

---

[10] Equality Act, s 26(3)(c).

[11] Equality Act, s 26(1)(b).

[12] Equality Act, s 109(4).

[13] Elizabeth George and Karen Jackson, 'Employment rights and duties, statutory office holders, and volunteers', in Anthony Robinson, David Ruebain and Susie Uppal (eds) *Blackstone's Guide to the Equality Act 2010* (Oxford University Press 2021), [4.30].

[14] Equality Act, s 26(4). The UK focus on the reasonableness of the effect of the harassment arguably undermines the subjective test required under the FED.

[15] *Unite the Union v Nailard* [2018] EWCA Civ 1203.

[16] Government Equalities Office, *Consultation on Sexual Harassment in the Workplace: Government Response* (Government Equalities Office 2021), www.gov.uk/government/consultations/consultation-on-sexual-harassm ent-in-the-workplace/outcome/consultation-on-sexual-harassment-in-the-workplace-government-response (accessed 30 November 2021).

definition of disability itself is more restrictive in the UK, as it requires 'substantial and long-term adverse effect' on the person's 'ability to carry out normal day-to-day activities'.[17] The UK comparison demonstrates that the FED can provide a core of commonality while also allowing for jurisdictional variation. This is not to say that all EU member states will be so closely aligned – the common-law heritage of the UK and Ireland perhaps permits a closer resemblance than Ireland might enjoy with other EU member states.

The FED may also have an indirect impact beyond the EU insofar as it informed the framing of harassment under the CRPD.[18] However, the CRPD does not yet appear to have had a major impact on the adoption of disability harassment legislation. In a recent detailed study of all 193 UN members, Heymann et al found that 62 per cent of countries prohibited disability-based discrimination in employment in the broad sense, but only a third prohibited indirect discrimination and only 30 per cent prohibited harassment.[19] Furthermore, only 16 per cent of low-income countries prohibited disability harassment at work, compared with 59 per cent of high-income countries.[20] Where disability harassment legislation exists, it may be unrelated to the CRPD. For instance, the US has not ratified the CRPD, but adopted the ADA in 1990, which has been used to ground disability harassment cases based on discrimination.[21] In Australia, the Disability

---

[17] Equality Act, s 6(1)(b).

[18] See Section 2.4.

[19] Jody Heymann, Elizabeth Wong and Willetta Waisath, 'A comparative overview of disability-related employment laws and policies in 193 countries' (2021) *Journal of Disability Policy Studies*, https://disabilityincl usiveemployment.org/wp-content/uploads/2021/05/heyman-2021.pdf (accessed 18 January 2022).

[20] Ibid, 5.

[21] Weber notes that US courts have overlooked an explicit provision in the ADA (s 12203(b) of title 42) that could be used to address disability harassment, relying instead on parallels with Title VII of the Civil Rights

Discrimination Act 1992 (Cth) pre–dates ratification of the CRPD and also prohibits disability harassment in employment. However, it does not define harassment, simply stating that it is unlawful to harass someone 'in relation to the disability'.[22] All this suggests that disability harassment legislation may vary significantly at the international level, even where states have ratified the CRPD. The Irish model may therefore have little comparative relevance for some jurisdictions in terms of the substantive content and legislative expression, particularly outside the EU.

6.2.3 Overarching structure

Like many jurisdictions, the overarching structure of the Irish model is one of individual enforcement. There is no general employer duty to combat harassment in Ireland. It is true that the reasonable steps defence in the EEA requires employers to demonstrate that they have done what could reasonably be expected, either to prevent harassment from occurring or to address it where it is brought to their attention. This generally merely requires employers to adopt a suitable harassment policy and implement an appropriate complaint and investigation process.[23] However, the reasonable steps requirement is not a positive duty that all employers must comply with, but simply a defence where an individual complainant alleges that harassment has occurred in a particular employment. Outside of this context, there is no obligation on most employers in Ireland to do anything to combat

---

Act 1964. Mark C. Weber, *Disability Harassment* (New York University Press 2007), 11.

[22] Disability Discrimination Act 1992 (Cth), s 35.

[23] For a full discussion, see Maeve Regan and Ailbhe Murphy, 'Employment equality', in Ailbhe Murphy and Maeve Regan (eds) *Employment Law* (2nd edn) (Bloomsbury Professional 2017), [17.54]–[17.64].

harassment[24] and no sanction for failing to do so. A similar approach is also evident in some other jurisdictions, for example, 'reasonable steps' defences are found in the Australian Sex Discrimination Act 1984 (Cth) in relation to claims of sexual harassment,[25] as well as in the Equality Act in the UK.

Several other key aspects of the overarching structure may be highlighted. First, the Irish model relies on a relatively informal tribunal system, rather than a more traditional court structure. Some other jurisdictions, such as the UK, have similar tribunal systems, though there may be significant variations in the systems adopted. While mediation is not mandatory, it nevertheless forms an important part of the Irish resolution system and is strongly encouraged; again, this is not unusual, though approaches vary in different jurisdictions.[26] Clearly, different resolution models may impact on outcomes.

Second, the operation of the burden of proof has a significant impact on the success of disability harassment cases in Ireland. As noted previously,[27] many complainants do not manage to reach the threshold of demonstrating a prima facie case, meaning that their case will not be considered further. This feature has a potentially broader application, as the burden of proof requirements apply in all EU member states. While this suggests a certain uniformity, a recent report by the EU Commission found that the burden of proof was often applied inconsistently by different national courts.[28]

---

[24] The public sector equality duty under s 42(1) of the Irish Human Rights and Equality Commission Act 2014 does not apply to private sector employers.

[25] Sex Discrimination Act 1984 (Cth), s 106(2). There is no similar defence in the Disability Discrimination Act 1992 (Cth).

[26] For example, before a case can be brought to the UK Employment Tribunal, it is mandatory to give notice to the ACAS in order to attempt early conciliation: Employment Tribunals Act 1996, s.18(1)(e).

[27] See Section 5.4.

[28] European Commission, 'Report on the application of Council Directive 2000/43/EC implementing the principle of equal

Third, difficulties arising from the very short time limit for complaints may also apply more broadly. In her recent analysis of age discrimination cases in Australia, Blackham also highlights short time limits as a key issue.[29] In the UK, the time limit is currently only three months, which has led to significant problems in practice.[30]

Fourth, the general lack of legal aid for equality cases in Ireland, and the impact of this on levels of representation, may have broader relevance. As noted previously,[31] it was difficult to establish the effect of legal representation on Irish case outcomes, as so few cases were successful. However, it was apparent that employers had significantly higher levels of representation (if not always legal representation). Similar concerns have been highlighted elsewhere: for example, in its report on sexual harassment in the UK, the Women and Equalities Committee noted that employees were almost always disadvantaged in relation to representation compared with employers and were often deterred from bringing claims.[32] Access to representation was also identified as central to the vindication of rights by the AHRC in its 2020 report on sexual harassment.[33]

---

treatment between persons irrespective of racial or ethnic origin ("the Racial Equality Directive") and of Council Directive 2000/78/EC establishing a general framework for equal treatment in employment and occupation ("the Employment Equality Directive")' (Com No. 139 final, 2021), [2.2.2].

[29] Alysia Blackham, 'Why do employment age discrimination cases fail? An analysis of Australian case law' (2020) 42 *Sydney Law Review*, 1, 16.

[30] Alysia Blackham, 'Enforcing rights in employment tribunals: insights from age discrimination claims in a new "dataset"' (2021) 41 *Legal Studies*, 390, 401–2.

[31] See Section 5.9.4.

[32] Women and Equalities Committee, *Sexual Harassment in the Workplace* (HC 2017–19, 725-I), 29.

[33] AHRC, *Respect@Work: Sexual Harassment National Inquiry Report* (AHRC 2020), 767.

Fifth, both the FED and the CRPD require that sanctions should be 'effective, proportionate and dissuasive'.[34] This requires not only adequate financial compensation, but potentially also other remedies, such as orders to take a particular course of action. The Irish findings demonstrated some use of non-financial remedies aimed at addressing structural inequalities,[35] though the low number of successful cases meant that this analysis was unfortunately limited. There are also no data on how effective these remedies were in practice. The broad scope of potential remedies in Ireland is not universally applicable; for instance, the UK removed previous legislative provisions that permitted wider recommendations to the employer[36] and recently decided against reversing this.[37]

6.2.4 Real-life results

It is remarkable how the Irish findings echo those in other jurisdictions, in terms of the low number of cases, the lack of success of cases at hearing and the reasons for case failure. While the international equality data are patchy,[38] the information available indicates that the high international prevalence of disability harassment is not reflected in the number of legal complaints[39] and that discrimination claims have a relatively low success rate across jurisdictions.[40] International research indicates that victims of discrimination are unlikely to take legal action, or even to make formal complaints, owing to

---

[34] FED, Art 17; UN Committee on the Rights of Persons with Disabilities, 'General Comment No. 6 (2018) on equality and non-discrimination' (2018) UN Doc CRPD/C/GC/6, [31(f)].

[35] See Section 5.8.

[36] Equality Act, s 124(3)(b), removed in 2015.

[37] Government Equalities Office, in note 16, [4.5].

[38] See Section 3.3.

[39] See Section 3.2.

[40] See Section 3.3.

multiple social and structural barriers.[41] The low rate of success in legal cases applies both to discrimination claims in the general sense and to disability discrimination and harassment claims specifically.[42] While there were variations – for instance, disability discrimination cases were significantly less successful in the US than in the UK – the overall picture was one of comparative failure. The international data also indicate an even lower rate of success for claims based on multiple discriminatory grounds. All this indicates that Ireland is not an outlier with regard to the low number of legal complaints and the very low success rate, including for multiple and intersectional claims. Rather, these findings reflect systemic factors, at least some of which may have more general relevance.

In terms of the reasons for case failure, the literature suggests some variation across jurisdictions. Disability harassment cases in the US appear largely to founder on restrictive judicial interpretations and standards.[43] Australia and the UK have little data on disability harassment cases specifically, but data on other kinds of discrimination cases bear a strong resemblance to the Irish findings. For instance, Blackham's work on age discrimination in Australia and the UK, drawing on extensive data sets in each jurisdiction, highlights very similar issues to those arising in the Irish context.[44] These include short time limits, problems with proof and causation, difficulties arising from evidentiary gaps, and claims that do not fall within the scope of the legislation.[45] Lockwood and Marda's analysis of

---

[41] See Section 3.2.

[42] See Section 3.3.

[43] Weber, in note 21, 11.

[44] See Section 3.3.

[45] Konur's earlier analysis of the operation of the UK Disability Discrimination Act 1995 also indicated a high level of case failure for jurisdictional and procedural reasons, as well as issues relating to tests for disability. Ozcan Konur, 'A judicial outcome analysis of the Disability Discrimination Act: a windfall for employers?' (2007) 22 *Disability & Society*, 187.

outcomes in harassment claims in the UK, though not disability specific, identified several reasons for failure that also arose under the EEA. These included a lack of detail or supporting evidence, failure to complain, bringing additional complaints, and sufficient steps having been taken by the employer.[46]

Overall, it may be said that the Irish experience tends to confirm the available international data on the relatively low effectiveness of equality law generally and of disability harassment law specifically. However, this lesson comes with a number of caveats, arising from differences in legislative content and overarching structure, particularly outside the EU.

6.3 Intersectional forms of harassment

The second lesson from experience concerns the wider implications of the Irish findings regarding intersectional forms of harassment. The findings might suggest that failure to address intersectionality is not of major importance. Although the Irish data showed that multiple grounds of discrimination were often initially alleged, they revealed few cases where specifically intersectional forms of harassment were identifiable. This finding is at odds with the international research, which indicates that intersectional forms of harassment are particularly significant for persons with disabilities.[47]

This apparent discrepancy is not unique to Ireland. For instance, O'Connell notes that Australian data indicate that sexual harassment is more prevalent in relation to persons with disabilities but that 'these prevalence rates are not reflected in publicly available Australian complaints data ... or in case law'.[48] Similarly, Blackham and Temple highlight 'the very

---

[46] Graeme Lockwood and Vidushi Marda, 'Harassment in the workplace: the legal context' (2014) 31 *Jurisprudence*, 667, 672.

[47] See Section 1.3.

[48] Karen O'Connell, 'Can law address intersectional sexual harassment? The case of claimants with personality disorders' (2019) 8 *Laws*, 34.

small number of cases that explicitly address intersectional issues' in the general Australian context,[49] despite finding, through detailed empirical analysis, that '[t]hose who belong to multiple impacted populations are far more likely to report experiencing discrimination' and that 'this discrimination is likely to align with relevant protected characteristics'.[50] They consequently argue that focusing on individual protected characteristics leads to an underestimation of the discriminatory experience.[51]

One possible explanation for the divergence between the incidence of intersectional forms of disability harassment and its visibility in the case law is that complainants may tailor their complaints to fit with the legislative framework.[52] Claims involving intersectional or multiple forms of discrimination are much less likely to succeed,[53] suggesting that complainants may make a tactical decision to focus on a single discriminatory ground, ignoring or dropping others. Failure to legislate explicitly for intersectional claims may therefore contribute to the continued invisibility of intersectional harms. A further explanation is offered by Blackham and Temple, who suggest that '[t]hose who experience intersectional discrimination may also be less likely to engage with the legal system',[54] as they are, by definition, particularly marginalized. This suggests that framing legislation to allow for intersectional claims is not necessarily sufficient to address intersectional discrimination[55];

---

[49] Alysia Blackham and Jeromey Temple, 'Intersectional discrimination in Australia: an empirical critique of the legal framework' (2020) 43 *University of New South Wales Law Journal*, 774, 783.

[50] Ibid, 796.

[51] Ibid.

[52] See Section 5.9.7.

[53] See Section 3.3.

[54] Blackham and Temple, in note 49, 783.

[55] See further Shreya Atrey, *Intersectional Discrimination* (Oxford University Press 2019), 2–3, and ch 4.

rather, specific attention must also be paid to addressing and removing systemic barriers.[56] In the case of sexual harassment of women with disabilities, for example, this might require us to address specific barriers to reporting (such as inaccessibility), as well as particular stereotypes and stigmas within the social and legal system (for example, regarding the credibility of women with psychosocial conditions).[57] The low success rate for multiple discrimination claims in Ireland (which accords with the international data)[58] also suggests other systemic problems, where adjudicators may be resistant to more complex claims.[59]

The significant lesson from experience in relation to intersectional discrimination may relate to transparency and barriers. We do not know what we need to address without measuring the extent of the problem – but we cannot measure what we cannot observe, and what we can observe is determined by how our system is structured. It follows that until we make it possible to frame claims in intersectional terms and to succeed in those claims, we will continue to screen them out, and we will not be able to see, evaluate or address the specific harms that many complainants may be subject to. This is particularly important in light of the CRPD, which requires states to address intersectional forms of discrimination, including harassment.[60] The CRPD also highlights the importance of continued monitoring to ensure that its goals are being met. However, although the CRPD Committee has repeatedly emphasized the need to adopt measures to address intersectional and multiple forms of discrimination in

---

[56] See Section 3.2.

[57] Rosario Grima Algora and Purna Sen, *Sexual Harassment against Women with Disabilities in the Work Place and on Campus* (UN Women 2020); O'Connell, in note 48.

[58] See Section 3.3.

[59] See, for example, Lockwood and Marda, in note 46, 672.

[60] See Section 2.3.

its concluding observations to states parties,[61] it has generally not addressed intersectional forms of work-related harassment specifically.[62]

A detailed discussion of how equality legislation can best be framed to address intersectional forms of discrimination is beyond the scope of this book, and indeed considerable work has already been done in this regard.[63] However, it is worth highlighting new ways in which the ILO Convention may be able to contribute to this debate. Although not yet widely ratified, the convention is unique in its insistence on the importance of an intersectional approach when trying to address work-related harassment.[64] Its accompanying Recommendation No. 206 also highlights the importance of multiple, parallel approaches in addressing harassment, for example, through occupational health and safety law, as well as anti-discrimination law.[65] By recharacterizing freedom from harassment as a general human right *as well as* an equality issue, the convention offers an alternative approach that may avoid the need to fit harassment claims into narrow

---

[61] See, for example, Committee on the Rights of Persons with Disabilities, 'Concluding observations on the combined second and third periodic reports of Australia' (CRPD/C/AUS/CO/2-3), [9]; Committee on the Rights of Persons with Disabilities, 'Concluding observations on the initial report of South Africa' (CRPD/C/ZAF/CO/1), [8(c)].

[62] The CRPD Committee has highlighted that women with disabilities are more at risk of harassment and other forms of gender-based violence but has referenced work-related disability harassment on only a handful of occasions. See, for example, Committee on the Rights of Persons with Disabilities, 'Concluding observations on the initial report of India' (CRPD/C/IND/CO/1), [57]; Committee on the Rights of Persons with Disabilities, 'Concluding observations on the initial report of Mexico' (CRPD/C/MEX/CO/1), [52(b)].

[63] See, for example, Atrey, in note 55; Blackham and Temple, in note 49.

[64] ILO Convention, Preamble, Arts 4, 6, 9. See Section 2.6.

[65] ILO, 'Violence and Harassment Recommendation' (2019) (No. 206), [2].

anti-discrimination frameworks. This may offer complainants greater freedom to present cases without tailoring them to fit within single protected grounds, or without having to explain potentially complex forms of intersectional disadvantage. There are, of course, potential downsides: a health and safety approach may fail to appreciate the kinds of harms that may arise due to inequality and othering (though it should be noted that bullying is addressed under health and safety law in many jurisdictions, including Ireland).[66] It may also fail to appreciate the structural nature of discrimination. However, as a parallel approach, it offers a potential means of overcoming some specific challenges and providing valuable support for complainants who may be particularly disadvantaged.

6.4 Addressing barriers to legislative effectiveness

Further lessons emerge from the Irish experience in terms of addressing barriers and improving the effectiveness of disability harassment legislation. Not all of these will apply to every jurisdiction; however, these issues have been identified in a range of jurisdictions, as well as in the general literature on harassment and equality litigation.[67] The comments in this section are limited to points deriving from the Irish case data analysis; many of the barriers identified in the general literature are beyond the scope of the Irish case analysis.

First, in relation to time limits, the Irish findings demonstrate that a short, six-month period for initiating equality claims can cause significant problems in practice. As short time limits are a recurring feature in equality law and are identified as a

---

[66] For a full discussion of the interaction of Irish tort law and statutory measures on bullying at work, see Maeve Regan and Ailbhe Murphy, 'Bullying, harassment and stress at work', in Regan and Murphy, in note 23, [8.10]–[8.20].

[67] See Section 3.2.

barrier in the literature,[68] it follows that a key step in promoting legislative effectiveness is to ensure time limits are adequate. This can be done in various ways. Increasing the time limit to initiate claims would allow longer for harassment victims to process trauma, consider options, obtain advice, enquire about dispute resolution methods and engage with employers and mediation. A longer period should operate as standard, rather than a short period with the possibility to apply for an extension, as the Irish experience suggests that complainants may be unaware that they can apply for this[69] and UK data suggest that, in practice, tribunals may be reluctant to grant extensions.[70] An alternative approach would be to suspend the time period while alternative resolution mechanisms are operating: for instance, the Equality Act in the UK provides for the suspension of the time limit during ACAS conciliation, though not during internal grievance mechanisms.[71] Failure to suspend the time period may encourage employers to 'run down the clock', yet complainants may be penalized if they fail to engage with employers or internal grievance mechanisms. The UK government currently proposes to extend the time limit for equality complaints to six months, following a public consultation[72]; while this may be an improvement, the Irish experience suggests that it may be insufficient to address this major barrier to successful claims.

Second, legal aid is generally not available in equality claims in Ireland, and employees have a significantly lower level of representation (of any kind) at hearing than employers. It is unclear how this affected the case outcomes analysed in this research due to the very low number of successful cases.[73]

---

[68] See Section 3.2.

[69] See Section 5.9.2.

[70] Blackham, in note 30, 405.

[71] See note 26.

[72] Government Equalities Office, in note 16, [3.4].

[73] See Section 5.9.4.

However, many reasons for case failure identified in the findings might have been pre-empted with proper advice, including: lack of evidence and proper record-keeping; failure to complain or to participate in internal processes; or failure to initiate legal claims in a timely manner.[74] It must also be noted, however, that representation is not only about successful outcomes. Rather, representation can also affect the ability or willingness even to bring a case, as an advisor can explain complex legislation, advise on rights and evidential requirements, complete paperwork and make oral arguments – all potential barriers to access to justice, particularly for members of marginalized groups.[75] Hence, a lack of legal aid can have a major impact on the effectiveness of legislation – a matter that has been highlighted by the CRPD Committee.[76] In this regard, the mere technical availability of legal aid is not sufficient; rather, thresholds need to be sufficiently low that members of marginalized groups can qualify for it.[77]

Third, specific training is recommended for adjudicators in relation to both harassment and intersectional discrimination. Failing to address intersectional discrimination is a significant legislative omission which has frequently been highlighted by the CRPD Committee.[78] However, simply amending national legislation to permit intersectional claims is unlikely on its own to be sufficient. As the Irish findings demonstrate (in line with international research), claims involving multiple

---

[74] See Section 5.9.2.

[75] See Section 3.2.

[76] See, for example, Committee on the Rights of Persons with Disabilities, 'Concluding observations on the initial report of the United Kingdom of Great Britain and Northern Ireland' (CRPD/C/GBR/CO/1), [33(c)].

[77] Women and Equalities Committee, in note 32, 29 (at [80]).

[78] See, for example, Committee on the Rights of Persons with Disabilities, 'Concluding observations on the initial report of France' (CRPD/C/FRA/CO/1), [11(a)].

and intersectional claims are significantly less likely to succeed. Various reasons have been suggested for this, including adjudicators' dislike of increased complexity.[79] Legislative changes should therefore be accompanied by specific training for adjudicators. This need is highlighted by Recommendation No. 206, accompanying the ILO Convention, which encourages 'gender-responsive guidelines and training programmes to assist judges, labour inspectors ... and other public officials in fulfilling their mandate regarding violence and harassment in the world of work'.[80]

Fourth, the definition of harassment may require clarification. As noted previously, the Irish definition of harassment as unwelcome behaviour related to a particular discriminatory ground has, in practice, led to a requirement to demonstrate a clear nexus between the complainant's disability and the offending behaviour. However, this requirement was sometimes misapplied to claims based on the general discrimination provisions, possibly as a proxy for comparison.[81] While further research is required to determine if similar confusion has arisen elsewhere, it is worth noting that the definition of harassment is drawn directly from the FED and, as such, may be replicated in other jurisdictions.[82] The Irish experience suggests not only that greater clarity may be required in legislative definitions of harassment, in terms of the criteria to be satisfied, but also that additional training or guidance may be required for adjudicators. The ILO Convention may again offer guidance here, through its expansive focus on actual or potential harm (including physical, psychological and economic harm), rather than the particular form that conduct takes.[83]

---

[79] Suzanne B. Goldberg, 'Harassment, workplace culture, and the power and limits of law' (2020) 70 *American University Law Review*, 419.

[80] ILO, in note 65, [23.b].

[81] See Section 5.9.5.

[82] As noted previously, the UK has a very similar definition.

[83] See Section 2.6.

Finally, the issue of monitoring has already been identified in relation to intersectional discrimination, but also applies to disability harassment cases generally. The low number of legal complaints going to hearing in Ireland and elsewhere makes it imperative to engage in greater monitoring and evaluation of equality case data. Notwithstanding the obligations in the CRPD and the strong recommendations of the European Commission,[84] states and national equality bodies have generally failed to monitor discrimination claims on a disaggregated basis. Without these data, it becomes impossible to know if legislation is being used, let alone if it is effective. The Irish example is a case in point: despite having comprehensive legislation on disability harassment for over 20 years, no official data of any kind are available on how much it is used and with what level of success. As a result of this information gap, the reasons for case failure have remained unexplored, and no attempt has been made by the state to identify or address the barriers to legislative effectiveness. Without sufficient transparency on the operation of the law, the underlying problems also become invisible, making it impossible to achieve systemic change.[85]

6.5 Moving towards positive employer duties

It has been argued that positive employer duties have the potential to reframe discrimination law by encouraging a more proactive approach that is less dependent on individual enforcement.[86] The CRPD recognizes a general state duty '[t]o take all appropriate measures to eliminate discrimination on the basis of disability by any person, organization or private

---

[84] Ibid.

[85] Alysia Blackham, 'Positive equality duties: the future of equality and transparency?' (2021) 37 *Law in Context*, 98, https://doi.org/10.26826/law-in-context.v37i2.150 (accessed 19 January 2022).

[86] Ibid.

enterprise'.[87] If disability harassment law based on individual enforcement is proving ineffective, arguably it is 'appropriate' for states to take further measures, including implementing positive employer duties, to combat disability harassment at work. Indeed, Art 9 of the ILO Convention also obliges states parties to adopt laws 'requiring employers to take appropriate steps commensurate with their degree of control to prevent violence and harassment in the world of work'. This includes a duty to 'identify hazards and assess the risks of violence and harassment, with the participation of workers and their representatives, and take measures to prevent and control them'.[88] It also includes the provision of training, in accessible formats, on the identified hazards and 'the associated prevention and protection measures'.[89]

6.5.1 Aspects of positive employer duties

Positive employer duties may take various forms, but two key aspects relate to organizational monitoring and cultural change. Organizational monitoring, which tracks harassment complaints and outcomes within the organization, is essential to identifying the prevalence of disability harassment and potential issues with internal resolution processes. However, organizational monitoring alone is insufficient, as meaningful change is unlikely without attention to organizational culture.[90] Blackham strongly argues in favour of increased transparency, including organizational monitoring, not as a substitute for other forms of regulation, such as anti-discrimination law, but as a complementary measure.[91] She contends that increased

---

[87] CRPD, Art 4(e).

[88] ILO Convention, Art 9(1)(c).

[89] ILO Convention, Art 9(1)(d).

[90] See, for example, Purna Sen, *What Will It Take? Promoting Cultural Change to End Sexual Harassment* (UN Women 2019), 35.

[91] Blackham, in note 85.

transparency would increase organizational focus on equality and discrimination, if only to avoid reputational damage.[92] As she argues:

> Positive duties – including duties aimed at increasing transparency – are aimed at achieving systemic and cultural change, including through the mainstreaming of equality. Ideally, this might mean there is no need for enforcement: if information is embedded and mainstreamed in organisational decision-making, addressing inequality will become part of how an organisation operates, without external prompting.[93]

By contrast, Allen contends that data collection alone is not sufficient without an obligation to address any inequalities revealed by that data.[94] At a practical level, it seems likely that the potential for enforcement would always be required to address inadequate compliance (as Blackham herself acknowledges);[95] a positive duty in the harassment context should therefore ensure that employers are required to collect appropriate data and to take steps to address any issues arising, even without complaints from individual employees. This would go beyond simply having an appropriate harassment policy and grievance procedure, as required by a 'reasonable steps' type of defence, and would encompass proactive measures, such as ongoing training. It should also, in Goldberg's view, focus on the development of an accountability culture within the organization, rather than tick-box legal compliance.[96]

---

[92] Ibid, 114. However, Blackham also argues that transparency duties are not feasible for small employers.

[93] Ibid, 104.

[94] Dominique Allen, 'Collecting, sharing and utilising data to inform decision-making and improve equality' (2021) 37 *Law in Context*, 88.

[95] Blackham, in note 85, 104.

[96] Goldberg, in note 79, 455.

Goldberg contends that employers shape workplace culture through procedures, operational decisions and training, and that these can be used more effectively to prevent harassment if they are not viewed merely as compliance concerns.[97] Although focusing on sexual harassment, her analysis is intended to have a broader application.[98] She argues that legal culture and workplace culture can 'reinforce or undermine' each other[99]: for example, legal accountability requirements can encourage supervisors and managers to address harassment.[100] Organizational policy and training can 'communicate organizational values to employees, whether intentionally or not, and will influence the ways that employees interact with each other, with spillover effects on the overall culture of the workplace, and vice versa'.[101] Arguing that 'legal-accountability culture is distinct from compliance culture',[102] Goldberg contends that workplace policy interventions, such as the provision of training, must be regarded as 'core to the organizational mission' if they are to send the right cultural signals within the organization.[103] She concludes that '[i]f law is to exert influence on workplace dynamics, workplace culture becomes a key site'.[104]

Seen in this light, positive employer duties offer potentially significant advantages over a purely reactive model. Since there is less reliance on individual enforcement, it is possible to mitigate the impact not only of many of the barriers to complaint,[105] but also of the barriers to successful case outcomes identified

---

[97] Ibid, 463.

[98] Ibid, 427.

[99] Ibid, 426.

[100] Ibid, 439–40.

[101] Ibid, 445.

[102] Ibid, 456.

[103] Ibid, 461.

[104] Ibid, 483.

[105] See Section 3.2.

in this research.[106] Positive duties may also, as Blackham argues, focus the attention of employers[107] and, in doing so, help to tackle some of the root causes of disability harassment, rather than dealing only with its manifestations.[108] The focus of positive duties is, then, systemic, focusing on organizational change, rather than individual transgressions.[109] Finally, increased transparency can also foster trust in organizational reporting processes if potential complainants see evidence of the appropriate and effective resolution of previous complaints at the organizational level.[110] This may, over time, help to combat at least some of the barriers to formal complaint.

6.5.2 Proposals for positive employer duties

Positive employer duties have recently been proposed in both the UK and Australia,[111] though Australia is not yet a party to the ILO Convention and the Convention will not enter into force in the UK until March 2023. The Australian proposals, which relate to the Sex Discrimination Act 1984 (Cth), are more detailed. This is primarily because of the concrete example of a positive duty in the state of Victoria. Victorian equality legislation obliges employers to 'take reasonable and proportionate measures to eliminate discrimination, sexual harassment or victimization as far as possible', taking account of various factors, such as the size and resources of the business, and the practicability and cost of the measures.[112] The Victorian Equal Opportunity and Human Rights

---

[106] See Section 5.9.2.

[107] Blackham, in note 85, 101.

[108] Bradley A. Areheart, 'Organizational justice and antidiscrimination' (2020) 104 *Minnesota Law Review*, 1921, 1924.

[109] Ibid.

[110] See, for example, Grima Algora and Sen, in note 57, 16.

[111] Government Equalities Office, in note 16, 10; AHRC, in note 33, 44.

[112] Equal Opportunity Act 2010 (Vict), s 15.

Commission has investigative and enforcement powers in relation to suspected breaches of the duty. The AHRC noted that the Victorian duty did not significantly increase the burden on employers, who already had to take steps to avoid being held vicariously liable for sexual harassment and had proactive health and safety duties under other legislation. It therefore concluded that a positive duty would not significantly increase the burden on employers and would offer significant benefits, as well as bringing Australian law into line with international best practice.[113]

The possibility of a positive duty has also been explored in the UK through public consultation,[114] to which the UK government responded in July 2021.[115] The consultation identified broad support for a new employer duty to take steps to prevent harassment.[116] The consultation proposal differed from the reasonable steps defence available under the Equality Act, as employers might be liable for breach of the duty to take preventive action even if no harassment occurred.[117] However, the government response stated that an incident of harassment would be required before an individual could make a claim,[118] suggesting some possible confusion.

Neither the AHRC recommendations nor the Victorian legislation reference organizational monitoring as a specific aspect of the employer duty. The UK consultation suggested monitoring and reporting mechanisms to increase

---

[113] AHRC, in note 33, 479.

[114] Government Equalities Office, in note 16. As the technical guidance on the consultation emphasized, the options explored in the consultation would apply to all forms of harassment, not simply sexual harassment, making it particularly apposite in light of the very low rate of successful complaints for disability harassment identified in this research, as discussed next.

[115] Government Equalities Office, in note 16, 5.

[116] Ibid, [4.1].

[117] Ibid.

[118] Ibid.

transparency[119] and stimulate company engagement at the senior level (presumably, organizational size criteria would apply). This suggestion was not addressed explicitly in the government response, though concerns were noted that publishing organizational data might create 'perverse incentives to drive down reporting figures'.[120] While this risk must be considered, the lack of any monitoring requirement represents a significant omission in the proposed scope of the duty. How can employers know what steps would be reasonable and proportionate to prevent harassment without accurate information regarding their current organizational context?

6.5.3 Enforcement

The other key question relates to enforcement. While compliance monitoring by a human rights body is particularly appropriate, it is clearly contingent on adequate resourcing, investigative powers and enforcement powers. Individual enforcement was suggested in the UK,[121] possibly in addition to conferring powers on the EHRC in a dual enforcement model. However, individual enforcement seems unrealistic given the reluctance of so many harassment victims to make official complaints, even when personally affected. The potential lack of compensation for complainants who have not personally suffered harassment must also be a significant disincentive to making complaints. The UK consultation also suggested a model based on existing penalties for failing to consult staff regarding business transfers,[122] but this did not receive a favourable response in the consultation.[123] A collective or trade union power of action might be more effective, but

---

[119] Ibid, 12.
[120] Ibid, [4.5].
[121] Ibid, 11.
[122] Ibid.
[123] Ibid, [4.1].

not all workplaces are unionized and increased union powers may not be acceptable in some political contexts. In the event, the UK government response to the public consultation suggested reliance on strategic enforcement by the EHRC and the development of a statutory code of practice to guide employers.[124] By contrast, the AHRC expressed confidence in its own ability to enforce the proposed positive duty, noting that this would complement parallel regulatory powers under health and safety legislation.[125]

Despite some challenges, a positive employer duty offers benefits to employers and employees, and is important for achieving organizational change.[126] Employers may identify and address important causes of workplace stress and dissatisfaction, and send an important message to their workforce, which may impact positively on organizational culture. Employees may feel that harassment is taken seriously and be more motivated to complain, where necessary. Where employees take individual legal action, organizational data might also be considered in relation to employer liability and the reasonable steps defence.

6.6 Conclusion

This chapter has argued that the Irish experience of the operation of disability harassment law has significant international relevance and offers useful lessons from experience. Irish law has similar objectives to legislation in other jurisdictions, particularly but not exclusively in the EU. Much of its substantive content and phrasing is derived from the FED, which has also informed legislative developments in other EU countries, albeit with jurisdictional variations. Key elements of the legislative and enforcement structure are also

---

[124] Ibid.
[125] AHRC, in note 33, 480.
[126] Ibid.

not uncommon in international terms, though there are many variations that necessarily impact on comparability. Available data also suggest that the low case numbers and poor success rate at hearing in Ireland are not unusual in international terms. There is also some international research with similar findings regarding the reasons for case failure. Overall, therefore, one important lesson from the Irish experience is that it tends to confirm the available international data on the poor effectiveness of equality and harassment law, and provides some indications as to the reasons for this.

The second lesson from experience is that intersectional forms of discrimination may be hard to measure or identify where legal systems do not readily facilitate or vindicate such claims. Structural factors within legal systems may affect how cases are presented and formulated, and this necessarily impacts on what can be observed. Ensuring that equality laws are formulated to encompass intersectional claims is therefore essential; however, a parallel route for claims through occupational health and safety law may also play an important role in overcoming conceptual challenges and practical barriers.

The Irish experience also offers lessons in terms of barriers to enforcement. These include the need for an adequate time period to initiate claims, including potentially the suspension of time to allow for internal processes and mediation. They also include the importance of supporting legal representation as a means of securing access to justice. Appropriate training for adjudicators in addressing intersectional concerns may also be necessary, as may greater clarity regarding the criteria for disability harassment. Finally, the importance of continued monitoring at the national level and the need for disaggregated data regarding the operation of disability harassment legislation were highlighted.

The chapter concludes by arguing that anti-discrimination law, which focuses on retrospective solutions and redress, and relies on individual enforcement, may be inadequate to meeting the challenge of disability harassment. Positive employer duties, including organizational monitoring, as well as training and other proactive measures, may offer an important additional contribution to changing workplace cultures, implementing structural change and combatting disability harassment at source.

SEVEN

Conclusion

7.1 Introduction

This book set out to explore the legal response to disability harassment at work. After outlining the nature of disability harassment and the intersections between disability harassment and other forms of discrimination, the book highlighted the global prevalence of disability harassment as a phenomenon that requires urgent legal attention. The available international research indicates that disability harassment is widespread and pervasive; it is also evident that persons with disabilities are particularly subject to intersectional forms of harassment, including sexual violence, in conjunction with such factors as race, gender, age and impairment type. However, although the human rights framework offers significant protections, particularly through the interpretations of relevant human rights committees, these are not uniform, and some important distinctions and gaps apply across contexts. This is likely to have a significant effect on the protection of human rights in practice.

7.2 Key issues with the human rights framework

This book focused particularly on the CRPD, FED and ILO Convention as the most significant instruments for addressing disability harassment in the EU and global contexts. It highlighted a number of important differences between these instruments, which have a considerable practical impact. First, the book highlights that the interpretation of disability under the FED is not yet fully compliant with that of the CRPD, notwithstanding a more expansive approach by the CJEU following the EU's ratification of the CRPD. This may result in significantly narrower protection under the FED, even within the limited context of employment. As discussed in this book,[1] the CJEU has, to date, failed to move fully towards the social model of disability enshrined in the CRPD, despite repeated references to the interaction between the impairment and 'various barriers'.[2] It remains unclear if the CJEU is willing to recognize purely social and attitudinal barriers, as opposed to physical ones or 'limitations' directly related to an impairment.[3] It also appears that disabilities under the FED must be at least potentially long-lasting,[4] even though the CRPD does not require this, but simply 'includes' long-term impairments within the meaning of disability.[5] The CJEU's emphasis on participation 'in professional life'[6] is also much narrower than the CRPD's emphasis on 'participation in society on an equal basis with others'.[7] The CJEU has rejected an interpretation of the FED that would encompass intersectional forms of discrimination and harassment,[8] resulting in a major

---

[1] See Section 2.5.

[2] See, for example, Joined Cases C-335/11 and C-337/11, *HK Danmark, Acting on Behalf of Jette Ring v Dansk almennyttigt Boligselskab and HK Danmark, Acting on Behalf of Lone Skouboe Werge v Dansk Arbejdsgiverforening, Acting on Behalf of Pro Display A/S (Ring and Skouboe Werge)* [2013] ECLI:EU:C:3013: 222, [93].

[3] Lisa Waddington and Andrea Broderick, *Combatting Disability Discrimination and Realising Equality: A Comparison of the UN CRPD and EU Equality and Non-discrimination Law* (European Commission 2019), 58. https://data.europa.eu/doi/10.2838/478746 (accessed 12 January 2022).

[4] C-395/15, *Mohamed Daouidi v Bootes Plus SL, Fondo de Garantía Salarial, Ministerio Fiscal* [2016] ECLI:EU:C:2016:917.

[5] CRPD, Art 1.

[6] *Z v A Government Department, The Board of Management of a Community School* [2014] ECLI:EU:C:2014:159, [80].

[7] CRPD, Art 1.

[8] Case C-443/15, *David L Parris v Trinity College Dublin and Others* [2016] ECLI:EU:C:2016:897.

compliance gap in relation to the CRPD. The danger is that EU member states may incorrectly assume that compliance with the FED is sufficient to meet their separate obligations under the CRPD, resulting in important gaps in coverage that are particularly pertinent to the issue of disability harassment. While the ILO Convention offers a more comprehensive, human rights-based approach to all forms of harassment in the 'world of work', it has not yet been widely ratified.

7.3 Key issues with national implementation

The primary issue with national implementation of disability harassment legislation is its apparent lack of effectiveness. Even where states enact legislation to address discrimination, a wide range of social and structural barriers discourage legal complaints and impede access to justice.[9] International research suggests that relatively few victims of unlawful discrimination take legal action, or even avail of organizational complaints mechanisms. There are many reasons for this, for example: low rights awareness; fear of not being believed; fear of retaliation or other adverse consequences; concerns about the adversarial nature of the system or the complexity of the process; lack of confidence in a positive outcome; and such concrete barriers as short timelines for filing complaints, inaccessible information and processes, and the likelihood of low compensation or ineffective remedies.

Even where legal complaints are brought, the available international data suggest that the rate of success is not high.[10] While the operation of disability harassment legislation in practice is insufficiently monitored, the available data indicate a consistently low level of success in equality complaints, including disability discrimination cases and sexual harassment cases. The limited evidence available from

---

[9] See Section 3.2.

[10] See Section 3.3.

a number of jurisdictions suggests that the success rate for disability harassment cases at hearing is particularly low, and this is confirmed in the Irish study. While it remains possible that the success rate may be higher for cases settled prior to adjudication (for example, through conciliation mechanisms), there are no available data on this. The international data also indicate that success rates for complaints relating to multiple and intersectional forms of discrimination are particularly low, and this again was confirmed by the Irish findings.

Analysis of the Irish cases identified a range of reasons for the high level of case failure.[11] Notwithstanding differences in national frameworks, it was clear that at least some of the issues identified have an international relevance. These include the failure to address intersectional forms of discrimination, short time limits for initiating legal claims, the lack of representation, the operation of the burden of proof and (potentially) the interpretation and application of the criteria for harassment. Additional research is required in relation to the operation of different national systems to explore this further.

7.4 Key recommendations for the future

While Chapter Six made some micro-level recommendations (such as longer periods to initiate legal claims),[12] the key recommendations of this book are at the macro level. These focus on three points: transparency, intersectionality and the need for positive measures.

7.4.1 Transparency

The first key recommendation relates to monitoring and data collection. Any analysis of the effectiveness of legislative

---

[11] See Section 5.4.
[12] See Section 6.4.

measures in combatting disability harassment at work is contingent on adequate data. Clear monitoring obligations are laid on states under the CRPD,[13] and the CRPD Committee has highlighted the need for ongoing monitoring and the availability of disaggregated data in its responses to periodic reports under the convention.[14] In his detailed exploration of monitoring under the CRPD, Quinn highlights the importance of monitoring to 'acculturation' and domestic reform processes,[15] noting that 'Rational policy rests on an accurate picture of the status of persons with disabilities'.[16] Monitoring and data collection are strongly encouraged by the EU Commission, though not required under the FED[17]; they are also required under the ILO Convention,[18] though this, as yet, has more limited application. The Irish case study is an example of what may happen when this monitoring and data collection is neglected. Despite having legislation in place to address disability harassment for over 20 years, and despite the full compliance of that legislation with the FED and its (almost) full compliance with the CRPD, the ineffectiveness of

---

[13] See Section 2.3.

[14] Committee on the Rights of Persons with Disabilities, 'General Comment No. 6 (2018) on equality and non-discrimination on Article 5', CRPD/C/GC/6, [34], [73(g)].

[15] Gerard Quinn, 'Resisting the "temptation of elegance": can the Convention on the Rights of Persons with Disabilities socialize states to right behaviour?', in Oddný Mjöll Arnardóttir and Gerard Quinn (eds), *The UN Convention on the Rights of Persons with Disabilities* (Vol 100) (BRILL, 2009), 224.

[16] Ibid, 254.

[17] The European Commission, 'Report on the application of Council Directive 2000/43/EC implementing the principle of equal treatment between persons irrespective of racial or ethnic origin ("the Racial Equality Directive") and of Council Directive 2000/78/EC establishing a general framework for equal treatment in employment and occupation ("the Employment Equality Directive")' (Com No. 139 final, 2021), [3.2].

[18] ILO Convention, Art 4.

the legislation in practice has never previously been identified.[19] As a result, no attempt has been made to identify or address the reasons for this failure. The Irish example also points to the need for data to be disaggregated. As the success rate for disability harassment claims was much lower than for other discrimination claims[20] – a finding that broadly aligns with the available international research[21] – it follows that data derived from harassment cases generally, or equality claims generally, cannot offer an accurate picture of the effectiveness of disability harassment legislation specifically. The first recommendation is therefore that states must design and implement appropriate collection processes for disaggregated data on the number of legal cases on disability, their outcomes (at adjudication or otherwise), the reasons for the success and failure of claims at adjudication, and the remedies applied. They must then monitor these data on an ongoing basis and respond to the findings.

7.4.2 Intersectionality

The second key recommendation relates to intersectional forms of harassment and discrimination. The Irish example suggests that it may be difficult to obtain a clear picture of the prevalence of intersectional harms unless legislation is framed to permit this type of claim. In other words, if intersectional forms of discrimination are not adequately addressed by national legislation, complainants may have to tailor their claims to try to fall within single protected grounds or do without a remedy. Intersectional harms may therefore largely remain invisible and unaddressed. Successful monitoring and data collection

---

[19] However, the caveats around the concept of effectiveness, discussed in Section 5.1, should be noted.
[20] See Section 4.6.
[21] See Section 3.3.

to guide policy development are thus contingent on systemic visibility. The second recommendation is therefore that states need to find ways to address intersectional harms. A multi-strand approach may be beneficial here, as outlined in the ILO Convention. This might include amending anti-discrimination laws to encompass intersectional claims, while also providing an alternative head of claim through occupational health and safety laws. It may also entail the provision of appropriate training to adjudicators and others to support the legislative application.

7.4.3 Positive employer duties

The third key recommendation relates to the need for a positive employer duty to combat disability harassment in employment. In light of the many barriers to enforcement and the poor outcomes in decided cases, it is clear that the individual enforcement model of equality legislation is deeply problematic. While it is important for anti-discrimination law to prohibit disability harassment (both to set standards for acceptable behaviour and because it may provide redress in some cases), it is evident that, on its own, this is insufficient to address the problem. Although multiple approaches may be identified to enhancing the effectiveness of equality law, [22] positive employer duties may help to address the underlying factors that contribute to disability harassment at work. Organizational culture is central to effective prevention and resolution;[23] however, the nature of a particular organization's

[22] Marie Mercat-Bruns, David B. Oppenheimer and Cady Sartorius (2018). 'Enforcement and effectiveness of antidiscrimination law: Global commonalities and practices'. In: Marie Mercat-Bruns, David B. Oppenheimer and Cady Sartorius (eds) *Comparative Perspectives on the Enforcement and Effectiveness of Antidiscrimination Law*. Springer, Cham.

[23] See, for example, Suzanne B. Goldberg, 'Harassment, workplace culture, and the power and limits of law' (2020) 70 *American University Law Review*, 419.

culture cannot be known without monitoring and reporting on internal complaints processes and their outcomes. It is also essential to engage with members of the workforce, through culture surveys and other means, to help identify problems. Employers should then be required to take reasonable steps to address any equality issues that come to light (even without individual complaints) and to engage in general pre-emptive measures, such as the provision of appropriate training. For practical reasons, these duties might be subject to organizational size criteria[24]; they should also be enforceable by adequately resourced national human rights bodies or regulatory agencies to avoid the recurring problems with individual complaints.

7.5 Conclusion

The final conclusion offered by this book is that while human rights frameworks may offer detailed guidance for combatting disability harassment at work, these are not always effective when implemented at the national level. Differences between frameworks may potentially lead to confusion, with a prime example in the EU context being the discrepancies between the CRPD and the FED. However, without adequate information – which must be disaggregated – we simply cannot know what is happening 'on the ground'. Quite apart from the operational issues identified here, national implementing measures have traditionally relied primarily on individual enforcement to provide redress for disability harassment, yet it is clear that multiple barriers operate to discourage and prevent this in practice. National measures may also often fail to address intersectional forms of discrimination, thus failing to comply fully with human rights requirements. This book

---

[24] Alysia Blackham, 'Positive equality duties: the future of equality and transparency?' (2021) 37 *Law in Context*, 98, 114, https://doi.org/10.26826/law-in-context.v37i2.150 (accessed 19 January 2022).

therefore argues not only for revised national frameworks that are in compliance with human rights requirements, but also for continued monitoring and increased transparency to enable barriers to be identified and addressed, as well as for positive employer duties to combat disability harassment at source.

Index

References to notes show both the page number
and the note number (101n18).

A

abuse 33
  Art 16 CRPD 56n166
  domestic abuse 80
  reporting 82
  sexual 30
  against women/girls with
      disabilities 34, 70
adjudicators
  claimant's credibility, view on 75
  rejection of claims, reasons
      for 108–16, 140
  training for 157–9, 167, 175
Allen, Dominique 161
Allott, Anthony 59, 97, 101n18
alternative dispute
      resolution 71, 98
anti-discrimination legislation 36,
      53, 56, 64, 154–5, 160,
      167, 175
Areheart, Bradley A. 62
*Asma Bougnaoui and Association
    de Défense des Droits de
    l'Homme (ADDH) v Micropole
    SA* 42
Atrey, Shreya 10–11, 23–4, 28,
      41, 139n148
attitudinal barriers, to legal
      complaints 46, 64–5,
      66, 76
Australia
  age discrimination
      claims in 72–3, 148
  Disability Discrimination Act
      1992 (Cth) 145–6
  Equal Opportunity Act 2010
      (Vict) 163–4

harassment in
  intersectional forms of 18, 151–2
  effectiveness of legislation 3
  positive employer duties, proposal
      for 163–4
  rate of success for claims 72–3,
      150
  'reasonable steps' defences 147
  Sex Discrimination Act 1984
      (Cth) 147, 163
  time limit for complaints 148
Australian Human Rights
      Commission (AHRC) 34,
      148, 164, 166

B

Bagenstos, Samuel R. 7–8
Barnett, Jessica Penwell 15
Barry, Brian 91–2n83, 92
behavioural impairments, and
      harassment 14
Beijing Declaration and Platform
      for Action 27
Blackham, Alysia 72, 73,
      148, 150, 151–2, 160–1,
      161n92, 163
Bornstein, Stephanie 64
*Bradford v Public Appointments
    Service* 112
Broderick, Andrea 43, 44
Buckley, Lucy-Ann 22, 45, 46,
      68, 70
bullying 16, 20, 61, 79–80,
      127, 155
burden of proof 36, 37, 38, 54,
      131, 138, 147, 172

C

Canada 16, 70n59
capacious approach, to
    disability 40, 42
CEDAW Committee 27, 29
CERD Committee 26–7
*Chacón Navas v Eurest Colectividades
    SA* 39, 47
*A Clerical Officer v A Public Service
    Employer* 111
Coleman v Attridge Law 38
Colker, Ruth 71–2
Committee on Economic,
    Social and Cultural Rights
    (CESCR) 27, 48
*A Complainant v A Third Level
    Institution* 115, 119,
    120, 125
complaints and legal claims
  barriers to legal
      complaints 60–71
    accessibility in relation to court
        procedures 66
    attitudinal barriers 46, 64–5,
        66, 76
    cost–benefit analysis 69
    due to non-identification or
        disclosing impairment 67–8
    EHRC's report on 67
    fear of loss of
        employment 68, 171
    financial burden 63
    ineffective remedies 64
    informational barriers 66
    in Ireland 81–2
    reasons for 62–3
    reliance on individual
        enforcement model 64, 73
    rights awareness, lack of 62,
        63–4, 76, 81, 82, 171
    specialized knowledge, lack
        of 66
    tribunal fees 65–6
  informal resolutions 61
  intersectional forms of
      harassment 75

success rates for equality
    claims 71–5, 76–7, 149–50
  adjudicators view on claimant's
      credibility 75
  in Australia 72–3
  and individual enforcement
      model of legislation 73
  in Ireland 93–5
  and time limits 73
  in UK 72, 73, 74
  in US 71–2, 74, 75
  see also reporting of
      discrimination/harassment
Conlon v Intel Ireland Ltd 115,
    119
Convention on the Elimination of
    All Forms of Discrimination
    against Women
    (CEDAW) 21, 28–9
Convention on the Elimination
    of All Forms of
    Racial Discrimination
    (CERD) 21, 26
Convention on the Rights of
    Persons with Disabilities
    (CRPD) 6, 21–2, 31, 51,
    52–3, 57–8, 142, 145–6,
    169–71
  compared with ILO
      Convention 53–6
  definition of disability 32, 35–6
  on disability harassment 33
  and FED
    distinctions between 23, 37–8,
        39
    interaction of 42–7
  focus on anti-discrimination
      law 53
  on harassment 32–3, 36
  on harassment in
      employment 33–4
  on intersectional forms of
      discrimination 153–4
  and intersectionality 34–5
  in Ireland 78, 88–90
  on monitoring 159, 173

multiple and intersectional
discrimination, distinguishing
between 35
on participation in society 44–5
recognition of general state
duty 159–60
remedies under 149
Convention on the Rights of the
Child (CRC) 26
Court of Justice of the European
Union (CJEU) 22, 170
and FED 37, 38, 39, 41
on long-term impairment as
disability 43–5
on medical model of
disability 45
on social model of
disability 42–3
CRC Committee 27
Crenshaw, Kimberlé 10, 11
CRPD *see* Convention on the
Rights of Persons with
Disabilities (CRPD)
CRPD Committee 32–3,
153, 154n62
on intersectionality 34–5
on lack of legal aid 157
on multiple and intersectional
discrimination 47
cultural change 160–2, 175–6

D

*David L Parris v Trinity College
Dublin and Others* 41,
42, 46–7
de Beco, Gauthier 26, 28
disability harassment
definition of 6
forms of 6–7
and hate crime 9
and human rights *see* human
rights framework
and intersectionality 9–15
in Ireland *see* Ireland
nature of 6–9, 20
prevalence of 15–19

disability harassment legislation 1
effectiveness 141–2, 166–8
barriers to 155–9, 167
intersectional forms of
harassment 151–5, 167
legislative purpose 142, 167
overarching structure of the
Irish model 146–9
positive employer
duties 159–66, 167–8
real-life results 149–51
substantive content and
legislative expression 142–6,
167
national implementation of 171–2
see also Employment Equality
Acts 1998–2021 (EEA)
(Ireland)

E

*An Employee v A Chain of Retail
Stores* 118
An Employee v An Employer 117
employers
development of accountability
culture 161–2
mandatory disclosure
requirements for 64
positive employer duties
see positive employer duties
Employment Equality Acts
1998–2021 (EEA)
(Ireland) 78, 83, 95–6,
97–101, 139–40
burden of proof 147
definition of
harassment 143, 158
facilitative effectiveness 101
unsuccessful cases 107–8
failure of cases, reasons
for 108–16, 151
adjudicator's preference 114
behaviour did not constitute
harassment 110
complainant did not
appear 116

complainant failed to
complain 113–14
complainant's credibility 116
complainants failed to notify
disabilities 114
complainant's failure to
complain 115
harassment as normal business
behaviour 76, 111
insufficient evidence 112–13
jurisdiction, lack of 113
nexus, lack of 111–12,
136–7
prima facie case, lack of 110
reasonable steps defence 137–8
intersectional discrimination
under 90
intersectional harassment 121–7,
138–9
age 126
gender 123, 126–7
pregnancy 123, 125–6
race 123
sexual harassment 85–6, 123
multiple discrimination 138–9
number of cases indicator 101–3,
105, 128–9
rate of success indicator 102,
105, 106–8, 129–32
'reasonable steps'
defence 137–8
related hypotheses 102–3
remedies under 87–8, 102, 127,
132–3, 149
statutory basis of claims 136–7
successful cases 106–7
successful cases, reasons
for 116–20
behaviour constituted
harassment 118, 119–20
clear nexus with
disability 118–19, 136–7
existence of a *prima facie*
case 116, 120, 131–2
nature of the behaviour 116
policy and procedural failings
by employers 116

policy or procedural
gaps 117–18
quality or quantity of the
evidence 116–17
EU law 4–5, 23, 31
under CRPD 42
and Employment Equality Acts
1998–2021 (EEA) 88–9,
92, 131
under FED 36–42, 79
European Commission 147, 173
on burden of proof 38
equality Directives 40
on lack of legal complaints 63–4
and monitoring and
reporting 159
report on the Race Directive and
the FED 61–2
European Convention on
Human Rights
(ECHR) 21, 25–6
European Court of Human
Rights 22, 25–6, 30

F

FED *see* Framework Employment
Directive (FED)
Fevre, Ralph 66–7, 68
Flynn, Eilionóir 66
*FOA Acting on Behalf of Karsten
Kaltoft* 43
*Food and Beverage Assistant v A
Hotel* 125
Framework Employment Directive
(FED) 21, 22–3, 31, 36,
52–3, 57–8, 142, 166,
169–71
anti-discrimination law, focus
on 53
and CRPD
distinctions between 23, 37–8,
39
interaction of 42–7
definition of disability 39, 45
definition of harassment 38–9,
143, 158

direct and indirect discrimination
in 41
on disability harassment in
employment 36–7
ILO Convention, compared
with 53–6
intersectional discrimination
under 39–41
in Ireland 78, 88, 89
monitoring and data collection
under 173
remedies under 37, 149
substantive requirements and
legislative expression 143
UK law, compared
with 143, 144–5
UN treaties, compared
with 37–8
understanding of disability
in 45–6
Fredman, Sandra 10, 11, 40,
42, 75

G

gender-based violence 14, 20, 29,
33, 51, 154n62
Goldberg, Suzanne B. 161–2
Gough, Mark 71

H

Hall, Mark A. 100–1, 103
*Hannon v First Direct Logistics
Limited* 126
Harpur, Paul David 13
hate crime 5, 9, 33, 49, 83
Haynes, Amanda 83
Heymann, Jody 145
Hogan, Victoria 80
human rights framework 1, 2,
21–4, 176–7
Convention on the
Elimination of All Forms
of Discrimination against
Women (CEDAW) 21,
28–9

Convention on the
Elimination of All Forms
of Racial Discrimination
(CERD) 21, 26
CRPD see Convention on
the Rights of Persons with
Disabilities (CRPD)
European Convention
on Human Rights
(ECHR) 21, 25–6
FED see Framework
Employment Directive
(FED)
ILO Convention see ILO
Violence and Harassment
Convention 2019
International Covenant
on Economic, Social
and Cultural Rights
(ICESCR) 21, 24–5,
48, 53
and intersectionality
see intersectionality
key issues with 169–71
locating disability harassment
in 24–31
Protocol to the African Charter
on Human and People's
Rights on the Rights of
Women in Africa (the
Maputo Protocol) 21, 29–30

I

ill-treatment at work 66, 80
see also mistreatment at work
ILO Violence and Harassment
Convention 2019 21, 23,
31, 47–56, 57–8, 163, 169,
171, 175
on consultation with worker
organizations 56
CRPD, compared with 53–6
definition of harassment 158
on employee voice 56
on employer duties 160

and equality legislation
framing 154–5
FED, compared with 53–6
gender-based violence 51
harassment on women under 51
migrant workers protection
under 51
monitoring and data collection
under 173
multifaceted harms, recognition
of 49–51
multi-pronged approach
mandates 53
on perpetrators of violence and
harassment 52–3
on positive duties of states 51–2
recharacterization of
harassment 48
remedial actions,
emphasis on 56
on third-party harassment 50, 56
on training programmes for
adjudicators 158
workers from vulnerability
groups protection
under 50–1
working context in 54–5
on work-related
communications 48–9
work-related violence and
harassment as human rights
abuse in 53
individual enforcement
model 64, 73
intellectual disabilities 13, 70, 113
International Covenant
on Economic, Social
and Cultural Rights
(ICESCR) 21, 24–5, 48, 53
intersectional
discrimination 10, 100
under CRPD 35–6, 47
under EEA 90
under EU law 40
under FED 39–41
and human rights
framework 23–4, 26

and multiple discrimination,
distinguishing between 35
of Muslim women 10, 12, 30,
41, 42
intersectionality 9–15, 20, 46,
99–100, 174–5
age aspect 1, 9, 12, 14, 19, 20,
26, 30, 34, 37, 41, 68, 72,
73, 100, 104, 126, 148,
150, 159
gender aspect 1, 2, 11, 12, 14,
15, 19, 20, 26, 27, 28, 31, 34,
40, 41, 42, 57, 68, 69, 100,
104, 123, 126–7, 159
prevalence of 18
racial aspect 1, 2, 9, 11, 12, 14,
15, 20, 26, 31, 34, 40, 42,
57, 68, 69, 70n59, 100, 104,
123, 159
religious aspect 9, 12, 34, 37
sexual orientation aspect 9, 12,
15, 34, 37, 104
treaty committees on 26–31
see also intersectional
discrimination;
multiple discrimination
Ireland 78
adjudication officers
(AOs) 91, 93
alternative dispute resolution 98
Central Statistics Office
(CSO) 79–80
CRPD compliance 78, 88–90
disability and sexual violence
in 81
employment equality law
definition of disability 84
disability harassment in 83–8
harassment and sexual
harassment in
workplace 85–6
statutory defence 86
test for harassment in 86
time limit for claims 87
equality officers (EOs) 91
FED compliance 78, 88, 89
hate speech legislation 83

Labour Court (LC) 91, 92, 93, 103, 106, 107
legal aid system 92, 148
legal discrimination complaints in
  barriers to 81–2
  rate of 81
legal representation, significance of 92, 120–1, 122, 133–6, 148
  and lack of jurisdiction 121
  trade union representation 120–1
prevalence of disability harassment in 79–83
success rate for equality claims in 93–5
tribunal system 90–3, 147
  Equality Tribunal (ET) 91, 106, 107
  and legal representation 92
  legally qualified officers 91–2
  mediation service 91
  problems in relation to WRC 92–3
  Workplace Relations Commission (WRC) 91, 92–3, 103, 106, 107, 133, 135
  see also Employment Equality Acts 1998–2021 (EEA) (Ireland)

J

jurisdiction, lack of 113, 121, 131

K

Kaiser, Cheryl R. 65
Koch, Lynn C. 7, 65
Konur, Ozcan 72, 150n45
Kristina Blumberga v Kilbush Nurseries Ltd 116, 123

L

legal aid system, lack of 36, 66, 82, 120
  addressing 156–7

in Ireland 92, 148, 156
legal complaints *see* complaints and legal claims
legal representation
  significance of 92, 120–1, 122, 133–6, 148
  and lack of jurisdiction 121
  trade union representation 120–1
  and tribunal systems 92
limitation of the ability to function 43, 90
Lockwood, Graeme 74–5, 150–1
low success rate for multiple discrimination claims in Ireland 152–3

M

MacMahon, Juliet 82, 93, 128, 129, 131n125, 132, 134, 135
Maher v HSE South 110
Maputo Protocol 21, 29–30
Marda, Vidushi 74–5, 150–1
McDonald, Paula 61
McGinnity, Frances 79, 81
medical model of disability 25, 31, 45, 84, 89, 116, 131
Miller, Carol T. 65
mistreatment at work 7, 64–5
  see also ill-treatment at work
monitoring
  of cases 4, 52, 167, 174–5, 177
  and CRPD 36, 153, 159, 173
  European Commission on 159
  and FED 173
  and ILO Convention 173
  in Ireland 99
  by states 159
  of organizations 160, 164–5, 168
Moss, Karthryn 72
Mousmouti, Maria 59–60, 62, 97, 142
Mr L v A Manufacturing Company 111–12
Ms Bridget Connolly v Health Service Executive 126

multiple discrimination 10, 100
  claims, low success rate
    for 152–3
  under CRPD 35–6, 47
  under EEA 138–9
  under EU law 40–1
  and human rights
    framework 23–4, 26
  and intersectional discrimination,
    distinguishing between 35
Muslim women, intersectional
  discrimination of 10, 12, 30,
  41, 42

N

negative stereotyping 13
neurological impairment, and
  harassment 14

O

O'Connell, Karen 151
organizational culture 160–2,
  166, 175–6
organizational monitoring
  see monitoring
O'Sullivan, Michelle 82, 93,
  128, 129, 131n125, 132,
  134, 135
othering of persons with
  disabilities 8, 9

P

physical harassment, complaints
  regarding 74
physical impairments, and
  harassment 14, 107
positive employer duties 4, 141,
  159–60, 167–8, 175–6, 177
  aspects of 160–3
  enforcement 165–6
  proposals for 163–5
prejudice 7–8, 9, 17, 30, 32, 43,
  70, 80, 89
privileges 8, 11

Protocol to the African Charter on
  Human and People's Rights
  on the Rights of Women
  in Africa (the Maputo
  Protocol) 21, 29–30
psychosocial disabilities 6,
  11, 13, 19, 20, 69, 70,
  76, 81, 84, 106, 107,
  125, 153

Q

Quinlivan, Shivaun 22
Quinn, Gerard 173

R

Race Directive 61, 88
Rape Crisis Network Ireland
  (RCNI) 82–3
reporting of discrimination/
    harassment 15–16, 176
  barriers to 153
    EHRC on 63, 67
    fear of blame 76, 82
  influencing factors 66–7
  obligations 128n112
  problems with 82
  sexual harassment 68
  and transparency 162–3, 165
  under-reporting 61–2, 68, 83
    see also complaints and
      legal claims
*A Retail Manager v A Supermarket
  Chain* 111
Richardson, Brian 69
rights awareness 62, 63–4, 76, 81,
  82, 171
Ring and Werge 42, 43–4, 45
Rosette, Shelby 11, 75
Russell, Helen 81

S

Sally Dowling v Debenhams Plc 110
*Samira Achbita and Centrum voor
  Gelijkheid van Kansen en voor*

Racismebestrijding v G4S Secure Solutions NV 42
Schiek, Dagmar 40
Schweppe, Jennifer 83
Sea and Shore Safety Services Ltd v Amanda Byrne 118
A Security Guard v A Security Firm 118, 119
sensory impairment, and harassment 14
sexual harassment 14
  barriers to legal complaints 68, 69–70
  under EEA 85–6, 123
  intersectionality 11–12
  legal claims in UK 74
  reporting of 68
  under-reporting 63
  of women with disabilities 18–19, 153
sexual violence 9, 80, 81, 82, 169
Shaw, Linda R. 13, 16
single axis discrimination 11
social exclusion 7, 8–9, 13, 20, 31
social model of disability 31, 42–3, 45n121, 89, 170
social participation 6, 7, 9, 32, 39, 44, 46, 160, 170
A Software Engineer v A Respondent 111
stereotyping 7–8, 11, 13, 22, 51, 70, 76, 138, 153
stigmatization 7, 8, 13, 20, 32, 65, 68, 153
synergistic forms of discrimination 75

T

Taylor, Juandalynn 69
Temple, Jeromey 151–2
third-party harassment 50, 56
time limits for complaint 64, 72–3, 130, 131, 140, 148, 172
  addressing 155–6
  advice on 131
  under EEA 87

trade unions 92, 120, 130, 134, 135, 165–6
training
  for adjudicators 157–9, 167, 175
  for employers 160, 162
transparency 162–3, 165, 172–4, 177

U

UK
  Advisory, Conciliation and Arbitration Service (ACAS) 91, 147n26, 156
  Disability Discrimination Act 1995 72, 150n45
  Employment Tribunal 147n26
  Equality Act 2010 143, 144–5, 147, 156, 164
  Equality and Human Rights Commission (EHRC) 7, 12, 17, 67, 166
  legal representation 148
  positive employer duties
    enforcement of 165
    proposal for 163, 164–5
  rate of success for claims 150–1
  success rates for equality claims 72, 73, 74
  time limit for complaints 148, 156
  tribunal systems 147
  Women and Equalities Committee 148
UN Special Rapporteur on Violence against Women, Its Causes and Consequences 29
UN Women 14, 69
US
  Americans with Disabilities Act (ADA) 71–2, 74, 145–6
  disability harassment in 7, 74
  discrimination claims in 71–2, 74, 75, 130, 150

Equal Employment Opportunity
    Commission (EEOC) cases
    in 13, 16
intersectional discrimination
    claims in 75

V

verbal harassment, complaints
    regarding 74
visibility of disabilities
  and reporting of
    harassment 66–7
  and risk of harassment 12–13

W

Waddington, Lisa 43, 44
Weber, Mark C. 7, 8, 74, 130
Women and Equalities
    Committee 63, 148
women with disabilities 14, 20,
    29–30, 76

abuse against 34, 70
coercive control 70–1
prevalence of sexual
    harassment and
    violence 18–19
reporting of harassment 68,
    69–70
sexual harassment of 153
*A Worker v A Government
    Department* 108
A Worker v A Restaurant 110
A Worker v An Employer 119
work-related
    communications 48–9
Wright, Ronald F. 100–1,
    103

Z

*Z v A Government Department,
    the Board of Management of a
    Community School* 44–6